June 2003

ADVANCING ENVIRONMENTAL JUSTICE THROUGH POLLUTION PREVENTION

A Report developed from the National Environmental Justice Advisory Council Meeting of December 9-13, 2002

A Federal Advisory Committee to the U.S. Environmental Protection Agency

This Report represents the efforts of the NEJAC on the topic of Advancing Environmental Justice through Pollution Prevention to identify and discuss the myriad of opportunities in applying pollution prevention to benefit environmental justice communities. Aspects of the issues related to the relationship between pollution prevention and environmental justice are covered in a consensus report. The individual perspectives of each of the four stakeholder groups - communities, tribes, business & industry, and government- are also contained in this Report. The NEJAC would like to acknowledge the many individuals and groups that have already shared their experience and expertise.

The NEJAC is grateful for the contributions from the NEJAC Pollution Prevention Work Group with assistance from Ms. Samara Swanston. In addition, the NEJAC thanks the Chemical Engineering Branch of the EPA Office of Pollution, Prevention and Toxics for the picture on the cover of this report, courtesy of ArtToday (arttoday.com).

 **NATIONAL ENVIRONMENTAL JUSTICE ADVISORY COUNCIL**

July 9, 2003

Deputy Administrator Linda Fisher
U.S. Environmental Protection Agency
1200 Pennsylvania Avenue, NW
Washington, DC 20004

Dear Deputy Administrator Fisher,

On behalf of the National Environmental Justice Advisory Council (NEJAC), I am pleased to transmit to you the report entitled, *Advancing Environmental Justice through Pollution Prevention* (June 2003).

EPA, through its Office of Environmental Justice, requested the National Environmental Justice Advisory Council (NEJAC) to provide recommendations on the question:

> **How can EPA promote innovation in the field of pollution prevention, waste minimization, and related areas to more effectively ensure a clean environment and quality of life for all peoples, including low-income, minority, and tribal communities?**

In response to this charge, the NEJAC has developed fourteen consensus recommendations in three major areas: (1) Community and Tribal Involvement, Capacity Building, and Partnerships; (2) More Effective Utilization of Tools And Programs; and (3) Sustainable Processes and Products. These recommendations are the result of a deliberative process that involved input from all stakeholder groups, including communities, tribes, business and industry, state and local government, non-governmental organizations, and academia. These recommendations also were the subject of a NEJAC meeting that took place in Baltimore, Maryland (December 9-13, 2002).

The NEJAC's recommendations consist of the following:

Theme I: Community and Tribal Involvement, Capacity Building, and Partnerships

♦ Develop and promote implementation of a multi-stakeholder collaborative model to advance environmental justice through pollution prevention.

♦ Increase community and tribal participation in pollution prevention partnerships by promoting capacity-building.

♦ Strengthen implementation of pollution prevention programs on tribal lands and Alaskan native villages.

A Federal Advisory Committee to the U.S. Environmental Protection Agency

◆ Promote efforts to institutionalize pollution prevention internationally, particularly in developing countries.

Theme II: More Effective Utilization of Tools And Programs

◆ Identify and implement opportunities to advance environmental justice through pollution prevention in federal environmental statutes.

◆ Promote local area multi-media, multi-hazard reduction planning and implementation.

◆ Promote efforts to incorporate pollution prevention in supplemental environmental projects (SEPs).

◆ Provide incentives to promote collaboration among communities, business and government on pollution prevention projects in environmental justice communities.

Theme III: Sustainable Processes and Products

◆ Encourage "Green buildings," "Green businesses," and "Green industries" through EPA's Brownfields and Smart Growth programs.

◆ Promote product substitution and process substitution in areas which impact low-income, minority and tribal communities.

◆ Promote just and sustainable transportation projects and initiatives.

◆ Improve opportunities for pollution prevention at federal facilities.

◆ Identify opportunities to promote cleaner technologies, cleaner energy and cleaner production in industrial and commercial enterprises in environmental justice communities

◆ Optimize and expand solid waste minimization activities.

The NEJAC is pleased to present this report to you for your review, consideration, response and action. In addition, the NEJAC appreciates any assistance you can provide in processing the recommendations in this report through the Office of Prevention, Pesticides, and Toxic Substances with consultation as appropriate with the Office of Environmental Justice and other relevant offices.

Sincerely,

Veronica Eady
Acting Chair

A Federal Advisory Committee to the U.S. Environmental Protection Agency

TABLE OF CONTENTS

SUMMARY (v - viii)

PART I: CONSENSUS REPORT

CHAPTER 1: CONSENSUS CHAPTER (1)

- Introduction (1)
- Purpose of the Report (5)
- Background on Pollution Prevention (6)
  - Definition (7)
- Background on Environmental Justice (9)
- Pollution Prevention and Environmental Justice (11)
- Enforcement and Pollution Prevention (12)
- Precautionary Principle (13)
- Tribal Government and Pollution Prevention (14)
- Understanding Pollution Impacts (15)
- Toward a Multi-stakeholder Collaborative Model (21)
- Pollution Prevention and Environmental Justice Framework (26)

CHAPTER 2: CONSENSUS RECOMMENDATIONS (29)

THEME I: COMMUNITY AND TRIBAL INVOLVEMENT, CAPACITY
BUILDING, AND PARTNERSHIPS

- Recommendation #I-1: Develop and Promote Implementation of a Multi-stakeholder Collaborative Model to Advance Environmental Justice through Pollution Prevention. (29)
- Recommendation #I-2: Increase Community and Tribal Participation in Pollution Prevention Partnerships by Promoting Capacity-building. (31)
- Recommendation #I-3: Strengthen Implementation of Pollution Prevention Programs on Tribal Lands and Alaskan Native Villages. (32)
- Recommendation #I-4: Promote Efforts to Institutionalize Pollution Prevention Internationally, Particularly in Developing Countries. (34)

THEME II: MORE EFFECTIVE UTILIZATION OF TOOLS AND
PROGRAMS (37)

- Recommendation #II-1: Identify and Implement Opportunities to Advance Environmental Justice through Pollution Prevention in Federal Environmental Statutes. (37)
- Recommendation #II-2: Promote Local Area Multi-Media, Multi-Hazard Reduction Planning and Implementation. (39)
- Recommendation #II-3: Promote Efforts to Incorporate Pollution Prevention in Supplemental Environmental Projects (SEPs). (40)

- Recommendation #II-4: Provide Incentives to Promote Collaboration Among Communities, Business and Government on Pollution Prevention Projects in Environmental Justice Communities. (42)

THEME III: SUSTAINABLE PROCESSES AND PRODUCTS (44)
- Recommendation #III-1: Encourage "Green buildings," "Green businesses," and "Green industries" through EPA's Brownfields and Smart Growth programs. (44)
- Recommendation #III-2: Promote Product Substitution and Process Substitution in Areas which Impact Low-income, Minority and Tribal Communities. (45)
- Recommendation #III-3: Promote Just and Sustainable Transportation Projects and Initiatives. (46)
- Recommendation #III-4: Improve Opportunities for Pollution Prevention at Federal Facilities (48)
- Recommendation #III-5: Opportunities to Promote Clean Production and Clean Energy (50)
- Recommendation #III-6: Optimize and Expand Solid Waste Minimization Activities (53)

PART II: STAKEHOLDER PERSPECTIVES
CHAPTER 3: COMMUNITY PERSPECTIVES (59)
- Introduction (59)
- Understanding Pollution Impacts (60)
  - Health and Environmental Impacts
  - Societal and Developmental Impacts
  - Economic Impacts
  - International Impacts
- Enforcement Issues (65)
- Addressing Community Impacts Through Pollution Prevention (66)
- Areas Where Pollution Prevention Can Improve Environmental Quality (68)
- Capacity-Building for Effective Community Participation in Pollution Prevention (69)
- Community Recommendations (70)
- Conclusion (72)

CHAPTER 4: TRIBAL PERSPECTIVES (75)
- The Legal Status and Rights of Tribes (75)
- Tribal Pollution Concerns that Can Be Addressed by Pollution Prevention (77)
- Possible Approaches for Implementing Pollution Prevention In and Near Tribal Lands (80)

CHAPTER 5: BUSINESS & INDUSTRY PERSPECTIVES (83)

- **Introduction (83)**
- **Current Business and Industry Efforts (87)**
  - Multi-Media Approach
  - Area Wide Approaches
    - Removal of Regulatory Impediments to Pollution Prevention
    - Recycling and Reuse
    - Pollution Prevention Initiatives in Permits
    - Environmental Management Systems
    - Emissions Reduction in Trading Programs
    - Pollution Prevention Components in Enforcement Actions
- **Communications Initiatives to Provide Incentives for Pollution Prevention (92)**
  - Corporate Environmental Reporting
  - 33/50 Program
  - Information on Product Content
- **Collaborative engagement to prevent pollution (94)**
  - Brownfields Revitalization
  - Responsible Care
- **Voluntary efforts (96)**
  - Product substitution/clean production
  - Sustainable production/renewable resources
  - Energy Efficiency
  - Conservation and Green Space Initiatives
  - Sector Identification of "Best Management Practices"
- **Resources, Incentives and Capacity Building (98)**
  - Green Subsidies
    - Renewable Fuel Vehicles and Other Green Energy Incentives
    - Brownfields Redevelopment Incentives
    - Subsidies for Installation of Green Technology
  - Green Procurement and Recycled Content Mandates and Subsidies
  - Research and Development Assistance
  - Regulatory flexibility
  - Regulatory Focus
  - Information
- **Public Recognition (104)**
  - Government awards/communication of good practices
  - Stakeholder Group Recognition
  - Multi-Stakeholder Group Recognition
- **Facilitation of Collaborative Engagement (105)**
  - Interagency Working Group (IWG) Template
  - Supplemental Environmental Projects (SEPs)
- **Business Recommendations to Enhance Pollution Prevention In Environmental Justice Communities (108)**

CHAPTER 6: GOVERNMENT PERSPECTIVES (111)
- **Historical and Regulatory Footprints (111)**
- **Pollution Prevention and Environmental Justice (112)**
- **Questions and Resolutions concerning Pollution Prevention and Environmental Justice (113)**
- **Governmental Integration of Pollution Prevention and Environmental Justice (115)**
- **Federal Government and Pollution Prevention (116)**
- **State Government and Pollution Prevention (121)**
- **Local Government and Pollution Prevention (123)**
- **Tribal Government and Pollution Prevention (124)**
- **Governmental Partnerships (126)**
  - The National Environmental Performance Partnership System
  - Compliance and Technical Assistance
- **Pollution Prevention and Performance Measurement (129)**
- **Pollution Prevention Model (131)**
- **Conclusion (132)**

APPENDICES
APPENDIX I: POLLUTION PREVENTION AND ENVIRONMENTAL JUSTICE CASE STUDIES (136)
- CASE STUDY #1: HOUSTON SHIP CHANNEL SOURCE REDUCTION PROJECT (136)
- CASE STUDY #2: BALTIMORE PARK HEIGHTS AUTO BODY / AUTO REPAIR SHOP (139)

APPENDIX II: CURRENT POLLUTION PREVENTION MANDATES IN FEDERAL STATUTES (142)

APPENDIX III: POLLUTION PREVENTION PARTNERSHIP PROGRAMS (145)

APPENDIX IV: POLLUTION PREVENTION WORK GROUP MEMBERS (152)

NATIONAL ENVIRONMENTAL JUSTICE ADVISORY COUNCIL (NEJAC) ADVANCING ENVIRONMENTAL JUSTICE THROUGH POLLUTION PREVENTION REPORT

Summary

The National Environmental Justice Advisory Council ("NEJAC") is a formal federal advisory committee of the U.S. Environmental Protection Agency (EPA). Its charter states that the NEJAC is to provide advice and recommendations on matters related to environmental justice to the EPA Administrator. The EPA Office of Environmental Justice requested that NEJAC examine how the innovative use of pollution prevention can help alleviate pollution problems in environmental justice communities. This report and recommendations grew out of a fifteen month long examination of the following question:

> **How can EPA promote innovation in the field of pollution prevention, waste minimization, and related areas to more effectively ensure a clean environment and quality of life for all peoples, including low-income, minority and tribal communities?**

In response to the request from the EPA Office of Environmental Justice, the NEJAC established Pollution Prevention Work Group. This Work Group is composed of representatives of diverse stakeholder groups, including community and tribal organizations, business and industry, state and local government, and academia. In addition, the NEJAC conducted an issue-oriented public meeting on pollution prevention in Baltimore, Maryland on December 9-12, 2002. This meeting received comments on, discussed and analyzed innovative approaches to use pollution prevention concepts to advance environmental justice.

As a result of the above, the NEJAC is pleased to transmit this comprehensive report and recommendations to the Administrator of the U.S. Environmental Protection Agency. The report and its consensus recommendations reflect the consensus views of the diverse stakeholder groups represented on the Work Group and Executive Council. For purposes of the NEJAC report, pollution prevention is defined by members of the Work Group as mechanisms which protect the environment and improve the quality of life for disproportionately impacted low-income, people of color, and/or tribal communities by systematically reducing, eliminating and/or preventing pollution.

It is hoped and expected that a robust consideration on the part of EPA of the recommendations included in this report will advance the interests of pollution reduction and improved environmental quality shared by impacted stakeholders, the general public, the EPA and the NEJAC. This report works to identify and discuss the particular issues that this question raises when – as is often the case – those negatively impacted by pollution are low-income communities, communities of color, and American Indian tribes/Alaskan Native villages and their members.

This report consists of two parts. The first part is the Consensus Report and contains two chapters: a consensus chapter and consensus recommendations. This consensus report represents positions, which all the major stakeholder groups in the NEJAC have agreed upon, and provides context, background, premises, conclusions and series of recommendations. The second part consists of four stakeholder group perspectives, i.e., communities, tribes, business and industry, and government. Appendices, including case studies applying pollution prevention methodologies to environmental justice communities, are also included.

PART I: CONSENSUS REPORT
Chapter 1: Consensus Chapter
Chapter 1 provides an introduction and the purpose of the report. It then gives a background on pollution prevention and environmental justice, and describes how the two movements have and can work together, including through the development and implementation of a multistakeholder collaborative model. The chapter presents a framework for advancing environmental justice through pollution prevention, as well as an initial set of critical barriers.

Chapter 2: Consensus Recommendations
Chapter 2 outlines a series of fourteen consensus recommendations, which have been divided into three themes:
  I. Community and Tribal Involvement, Capacity Building, and Partnerships,
  II. More Effective Utilization of Tools And Programs,
  III. More Effective Utilization of Tools And Programs.

Theme I: Community and Tribal Involvement, Capacity Building, and Partnerships
- Recommendation #I-1: Develop and Promote Implementation of a Multi-stakeholder Collaborative Model to Advance Environmental Justice through Pollution Prevention. (31)
- Recommendation #I-2: Increase Community and Tribal Participation in Pollution Prevention Partnerships by Promoting Capacity-building. (33)
- Recommendation #I-3: Strengthen Implementation of Pollution Prevention Programs on Tribal Lands and Alaskan Native Villages. (34)
- Recommendation #I-4: Promote Efforts to Institutionalize Pollution Prevention Internationally, Particularly in Developing Countries. (37)

Theme II: More Effective Utilization of Tools And Programs
- Recommendation #II-1: Identify and Implement Opportunities to Advance Environmental Justice through Pollution Prevention in Federal Environmental Statutes. (38)
- Recommendation #II-2: Promote Local Area Multi-Media, Multi-Hazard Reduction Planning and Implementation. (40)
- Recommendation #II-3: Promote Efforts to Incorporate Pollution Prevention in Supplemental Environmental Projects (SEPs). (41)

- Recommendation #II-4: Provide Incentives to Promote Collaboration Among Communities, Business and Government on Pollution Prevention Projects in Environmental Justice Communities. (43)

Theme III: Sustainable Processes and Products
- Recommendation #III-1: Encourage "Green buildings," "Green businesses," and "Green industries" through EPA's Brownfields and Smart Growth programs. (45)
- Recommendation #III-2: Promote Product Substitution and Process Substitution in Areas which Impact Low-income, Minority and Tribal Communities. (46)
- Recommendation #III-3: Promote Just and Sustainable Transportation Projects and Initiatives. (48)
- Recommendation #III-4: Improve Opportunities for Pollution Prevention at Federal Facilities (49)
- Recommendation #III-5: Opportunities to Promote Clean Production and Clean Energy (52)
- Recommendation #III-6: Optimize and Expand Solid Waste Minimization Activities (54)

PART II: STAKEHOLDER PERSPECTIVES

Chapters 3-6 provide four stakeholder group perspectives on pollution prevention and environmental justice. These are community, tribal, business and industry, and government perspectives.

Chapter 3 gives an overview of the community perspective of understanding pollution impacts, including health, environmental, societal and economic impacts. Enforcement issues and current environmental controls are highlighted and provide a greater understanding of what has and has not worked outside of the field of pollution prevention. Areas where pollution prevention can improve environmental quality are discussed, as well as capacity building for communities to effectively participate in these pollution prevention efforts. A series of recommendations from the community perspective concludes this chapter.

Chapter 4 addresses the complex issue of the legal status and rights of tribes. Pollution concerns in and near tribal lands that can be addressed by pollution prevention and implementation of these pollution prevention projects are also reviewed.

Chapter 5 begins with current business and industry efforts to employ both multi-media and area wide approaches to pollution prevention. The next section addresses initiatives that provide incentives to undertake pollution prevention activities. Collaborative (Responsible Care) and voluntary (product substitution) efforts are reviewed. Resources and incentives for capacity building, such as green subsidies and regulatory flexibility are then addressed. The chapter closes with a section on public recognition, facilitating a collaborative approach, and the business recommendations to enhance pollution prevention in environmental justice communities.

Chapter 6 begins by reviewing the historical and regulatory footprints of the environmental movement. The next portion of this chapter addresses pollution prevention and environmental justice, including background, questions and resolutions, and governmental integration. Pollution prevention is then reviewed from federal, state, local and tribal government perspectives. The chapter closes with performance measurement and a model for pollution prevention.

CHAPTER 1: CONSENSUS CHAPTER

INTRODUCTION

The concept embodied in title of this report, *Advancing Environmental Justice through Pollution Prevention*, is part of a transition to a new vision of environmental responsibilities among business, government and impacted communities. As we move from our contemporary framework into new relationships, pollution prevention strategies and approaches can shift our limited resources into more productive, revitalizing work, strengthened from and enabled by participating community members. We can achieve benefits of risk reduction and secure the benefits of modernization in our most endangered communities by using this type of innovation in impacted communities to augment traditional environmental protection mechanisms. New technologies are available to build vibrant communities producing and using high quality, low cost environmentally sound products produced in an environmentally sound manner while providing jobs and engaging industry in bringing about real change. Environmental justice communities can serve as learning laboratories for constructive innovation.

Central to the transformations needed in the community are these paradigm shifts:
- The control of environmental contamination at the point of release to the prevention of pollution at the source.
- Continued exposure to the effects of sudden and accidental releases from industrial facilities to the prevention of these accidents by building inherent safety and sustainability into the process.

This requires technological, organizational, and work practice changes. The needed changes may involve more than the adoption of better off-the-shelf technologies and approaches. Innovation in the development of new products, processes, and approaches may be necessary. Still more dramatic changes may be required at the system level to encourage sustainable products and sustainable production leading to sustainable development. Communities and tribes, business and industry, and government are essential partners in this endeavor.

Administrator Christine Todd Whitman confirmed [1] EPA's commitment to environmental justice, saying "[e]nvironmental justice is the goal to be achieved for all communities and persons across this nation" and that it will be achieved when everyone enjoys the same degree of protection from environmental and health hazards and has a "healthy environment where they live, learn and work." U.S. Secretary of State Colin Powell's comments at the World Summit targeted poverty and destruction of the environment as issues that can destabilize nations and described sustainable development as a "means to unlock human potential through economic development based upon sound

---

[1] Christine Todd Whitman, Environmental Protection Agency, EPA's Commitment to Environmental Justice, Memorandum, August 9, 2001.

economic policy, social development based upon investment in health and education and responsible stewardship of the environment."[2] Secretary Powell described our time as a "century of promise" but cautioned that the great potential evident comes with a responsibility to turn it into a "century of hopes fulfilled and sustained development that enriches all people without impoverishing the planet."[3] Secretary Powell's comments identify the inherent challenge in using pollution prevention to advance environmental justice through sustainable development.

One of the most significant implications of the 2002 United Nations World Summit on Sustainable Development[4] is greater impetus for addressing both pollution prevention and environmental justice together. At the World Summit, participants agreed upon a Plan of Implementation that recognized the linkages among poverty, health and the environment in addressing environmental health threats, especially as they impact upon vulnerable populations. The implementation plan calls for "national initiatives to accelerate the shift towards sustainable…production by…de-linking economic growth and environmental degradation through improving efficiency and sustainability in the use of resources and production processes and reducing resource degradation, pollution and waste."[5]

Historically the environmental justice movement and the pollution prevention movement developed independently. Environmental justice advocates sought environmental improvements, despite resistance from critics who argued that environmental improvements came at a cost to economic growth. Preventing pollution was initially couched in facility specific and technical terms that left little access for non-technical members of impacted communities. Yet both movements have traveled similar roads. Over the last two decades both movements witnessed a surge of public attention and a substantial catalogue of successes in advancing their objectives. Both movements have also experienced change. The pollution prevention movement has experienced a slowing of progress as pollution prevention advanced to a point where more technical and complex efforts are now needed. The environmental justice movement has experienced refinement and maturation as it contends with the complexities of developing proactive strategies that effectively address a multiplicity of environmental, health, economic, and social concerns.

Over the past fifteen years a number of strategies have been proposed and / or implemented to reduce the impacts of pollution and improve environmental quality for tribal communities, low-income communities and communities of color. Some of these strategies were seen as ways to eliminate disproportionate environmental burdens and

---

[2] Secretary Colin L. Powell, Making Sustainable Development Work: Governance, Finance and Public-Private Cooperation, at p. 2, Remarks at State Department Conference, Meridian International Center, Washington, D.C., July 12, 2002.
[3] Id.
[4] The United Nations World Summit on Sustainable Development was held in South Africa in August-September of 2002.
[5] United Nations World Summit on Sustainable Development, Plan of Implementation, Advance unedited September 4, 2002 text, p. 5, III, Changing unsustainable patterns of consumption and production at pp. 14.

their attendant adverse health effects,[6] and have included executive directives and statutorily based strategies ranging from new state legislation to litigation using existing environmental and civil rights laws or regulations.

In addition, an ever-growing body of research has been accumulated from several programs initiated by both private and public entities, some concomitantly. EPA alone has a myriad of voluntary partnership programs that are based in pollution prevention principles and improved environmental management systems. Many individual major corporations and business organizations have undertaken important sustainable development initiatives. For example, in the United States the Global Environmental Management Initiative, a consortium of major corporations, developed tools for use by corporations managing their environmental issues, including guidance for addressing sustainable development, and The Conference Board has conducted and published research concerning corporate environmental management and corporate social responsibility. Internationally, the World Business Council for Sustainable Development, which includes U.S. as well as international corporations, has taken a leadership role in promoting sustainable development. Another important initiative involves representatives of major corporations, venture capitalists, and small companies, academic and non-profit organizations in looking at how to provide low cost, high quality, low environmental footprint products to poor communities worldwide.

While a variety of these strategies have been effective, environmental justice communities still need even more tools to eliminate and reduce toxic exposures. Nevertheless, exploring all of these strategies has allowed us to get to this point where we can more clearly see and capitalize on our opportunities. Today, there appears to be a host of benefits in promoting pollution prevention, especially as a means of achieving environmental justice objectives.

These are complex times for new initiatives and short-term trends are unsettling. The recent chilling of the recently robust economy means less available resources and more competition for a dwindling supply of public and private dollars. A heightened concern over terrorism and national security has re-directed government priorities at both the state and national levels. Longer-term structural shifts in the national economy also present major challenges. Increasing globalization with a transition from traditional manufacturing to services and information technology has emerged in developed countries and growing operations of transnational corporations across the world accompanied by a growing distance between those who are doing well and those who are not. Longer-term trends such as habitat loss and alteration threaten resource conservation, biodiversity and the benefits that result from it.[7] Climate change and fresh

---

[6] Executive Order 12898, Federal Actions to Address Environmental Justice in Minority Populations and Low-Income Populations, February 11, 1994.

[7] National Geographic News, Near Total Ape-Habitat Loss Foreseen by 2030, United Nations Environment Program, Great Ape Survival Project (The report, released at the World Summit on Sustainable Development, indicated that less than 10% of the remaining habitat of the great apes will be left relatively undisturbed if the road building, mining and infrastructure developments continue at current levels.)

water resources will also be a driving factor in the global economy in the immediate coming years.[8] These shifts are certain to affect the generation of pollution and wastes and on the prospects of those in indigenous and low-income communities and developing countries.

Amid such challenges appear a wealth of new opportunities that highlight the need for change. The growing importance of international environmental policies around chemicals, water use, waste trade, and climate protection[9] has created new influences in shaping environmental policy, and advanced the importance of establishing regulations to protect the environment and the public health. The importance of international markets has sharpened the global attention of national businesses. The emergence of interest in environmental justice around the world offers prospects for new energy and cross-national collaborations. A new business ethic that embraces environmental management as a core business objective makes pollution prevention and clean production and their associated economic benefits welcome values in shaping production and product design decisions.[10] There is also a new focus on the safety of plants that store and manufacture chemicals, measures that would require plants to look beyond traditional security measures and examine "substituting less volatile or toxic chemical for substances currently in use and storing less material on site." [11]

As evidenced by the above trends and other indicators, there exists today enormous opportunities to build upon the natural synergies between environmental justice and pollution prevention in areas such as community revitalization and sustainable development. Some of the most promising appear around Brownfields restoration and redevelopment; around "smart growth" and more integrated transportation and land use planning; alternative fuels, and around environmental management systems which are increasingly being adopted by leading businesses.

---

available at http://news.nationalgeographic.com/news/2002/09/0903_020903_apes.html; BBCI, State of the Planet, Habitat Loss (stating that half of the world's forest have been lost with the rate of loss ten times higher than the rate of regrowth, that one sixth of the world's living primate species will go extinct in the wild in the next 10-20 years and that the only species not truly affected by habitat loss are those which benefit from human activity such as cock roaches, rats and house finches) available at www.bbc.co.uk/programmes/tv/state_planet/habitat.shtml

[8] University of Cambridge, Climate Change...The Facts, What Can Be Done to Prevent Further Climate Change, Climate Change 2001: Mitigation ("The good news is that technological progress to reduce emissions or find new, non-fossil energy sources has been faster than anticipated in the second IPCC Assessment Report (1996). More efficient hybrid engines, wind turbines and elimination of some industrial by-product gasses are examples.)" available at www.alphagalileo.org/index.cfm.

[9] Id.

[10] David C. Lowy and Richard P. Wells, Corporate Environmental Governance: Benchmarks Toward World-Class Systems, The Conference Board, Inc., Townley Global Management Center (2000); David Champion, Environmental Management, Harvard Business Review (1998).

[11] The Washington Post, Editorial, Seeking Chemical Safety, September 14th, 2002 at page A20; Carol D. Leonnig and Spencer S. Hue, Fearing Attack, Blue Plains Ceases Toxic Chemical Use, The Washington Post, November 10, 2001 at p. A01.

Energy efficiency and clean production technologies also present real opportunities to address some of the challenges we face. These suggest rich prospects for creative and effective projects that can protect workers and the environment and contribute to job creation and retention in the United States. Rather than creating job loss or limiting economic growth, these projects strongly indicate that reducing pollution through measures that protect the environment provide economic benefits and have great potential for new job development. However, if such projects are to substantively promote environmental justice they need to build constructive partnerships, involve multiple stakeholders, promote local participation, protect communities and workers and provide targeted and measurable results.

> ... it has been suggested that the redevelopment of brownfields could serve as a check or constraint on urban sprawl by reducing developmental pressures on greenfields. This is an area of growing concern. According to the American Farmlands Trust, between 1982 to 1992, 13,823,000 acres of land were converted to urban use. Of this total, 4,266,000 acres were either prime or unique farmland.
>
> From the report. Public Policies and Private Decisions Affecting the Redevelopment of Brownfields: An Analysis of Critical Factors, Relative Weights and Areal Differentials (George Washington University, September 2001)

PURPOSE OF THE REPORT

The National Environmental Justice Advisory Council ("NEJAC") is the formal federal advisory committee on environmental justice. Its charter states that the NEJAC is to provide advice and recommendations on matters related to environmental justice to the EPA Administrator. The EPA Office of Environmental Justice requested that NEJAC examine how the innovative use of pollution prevention can help alleviate pollution problems in environmental justice communities. In response to the request from the EPA Office of Environmental Justice, the NEJAC conducted an issue-oriented public meeting in Baltimore, Maryland on December 9-12, 2002 and received comments on, discussed and analyzed innovative approaches to use pollution prevention concepts to advance environmental justice. In order to provide advice and recommendations to the Administrator in respect to ways that pollution prevention can advance environmental justice, the NEJAC has prepared a comprehensive report that reflects the diverse views, interests, concerns and perspectives of identified stakeholders on the focused policy issue. For purposes of the NEJAC Report, pollution prevention, as developed from interviews of the stakeholders, is defined as a mechanism focused on reduction, elimination or prevention that helps to protect the environment and improve quality of life in environmental justice and tribal communities. The question presented for analysis in this report is:

> **How can EPA promote innovation in the field of pollution prevention, waste minimization, and related areas to more effectively ensure a clean environment and quality of life for all peoples, including low-income, minority and tribal communities?**

5

A robust consideration of the answers suggested as a result of this inquiry should advance the interests of pollution reduction and improved environmental quality shared by the public, all stakeholders, the EPA and the NEJAC.

Since tribes are governments, since a tribe is generally comprised of one or more common ties (generally "of color" and low income), and since tribes frequently own business enterprises, each of the chapters in part II includes some discussion of tribal issues. Since many issues relating to tribes are more or less unique to them, a separate chapter on tribes has been included.

This report consists of two parts. The first part is a consensus report that provides context, background, premises, conclusions and series of agreed upon recommendations by all the stakeholders. The second part consists of four stakeholder perspectives, i.e., communities, tribes, business and industry, and government. In addition, the Report contains four appendices. The first contains two case studies applying pollution prevention to environmental justice communities. The second examines pollution prevention mandates in federal statutes, and the third lists pollution prevention partnerships. A list of the Work Group members comprises the fourth and final appendix.

BACKGROUND ON POLLUTION PREVENTION

Reducing pollution and improving environmental quality were initially accomplished though a variety of federal environmental statutes that protected public health and the environment by controlling pollution after its creation "at the end of the pipe". The focus of these statutes was not controlling the amount of pollution that was created but limiting how much was discharged into the environment. These statutes were implemented with varying degrees of effectiveness. However, industrial growth could not be sustained with the ever-increasing number of regulations limiting the amount of emissions to the environment even with the most advanced technology. Ultimately it became obvious that the regulatory control activities needed to be expanded to include innovative activities that address pollution prior to its release into the environment. This realization led to the formation and adoption of the Pollution Prevention Act in 1990. The Pollution Prevention Act directed that pollution should be prevented or reduced at the source whenever feasible. Instead of reiterating the "end of pipe" treatment of environmental pollutants, "pollution prevention" moved upstream to prevent the pollutants from being generated in the first place.

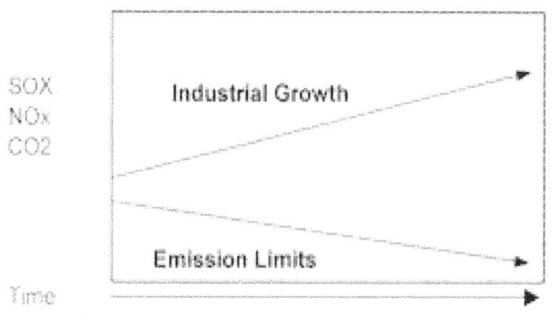 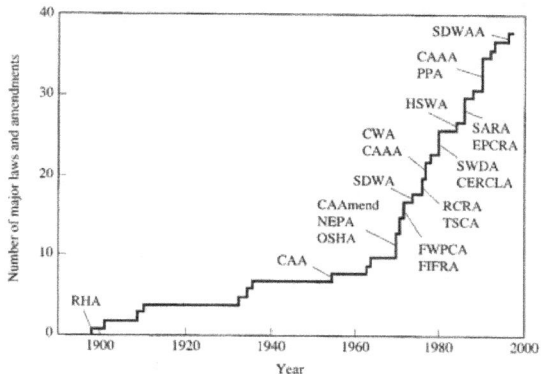

Definition

Pollution prevention ("P2") is the reduction or elimination of wastes and pollutants at the source. By reducing the use and production of hazardous substances, and by operating more efficiently, we protect human health, strengthen our economic well-being, and preserve the environment. Conventional pollution prevention encompasses a wide variety of activities including:

- More efficient use of materials, water, energy and other resources
- Substituting less harmful substances for hazardous ones
- Reducing or eliminating toxic substances from the production process
- Developing new uses for existing chemical-and process wastes
- Recycling and reuse
- Conserving natural resources

Reducing pollution at its source, or source reduction, allows for the greatest and quickest improvements in environmental protection by avoiding the generation of waste and harmful emissions. Source reduction helps to make the regulatory system more efficient by reducing the need for end-of-pipe [after generation] environmental control by government. EPA defines pollution prevention to mean source reduction, as defined under the Pollution Prevention Act, and other practices that reduce or eliminate the creation of pollutants through increased efficiency in the use of raw materials, energy, water, or other resources, or protection of natural resources by conservation. The term source reduction includes: equipment or technology modifications, process or procedure modifications, reformulation or redesign or products, substitution of raw materials, and improvements in housekeeping, maintenance, training, or inventory control. Therefore, pollution prevention as a strategy is more comprehensive and provides greater benefits than purely toxic reduction.

The process of pollution prevention involves identification, resolution, and action. First, government, business, consumers — society, in general — must identify the root causes and sources of waste and pollutants, and results should be measured. After identifying the sources, a decision must be made as to how best to minimize the generation of these wastes and pollutants. Assessing the efficiency, appropriateness, and feasibility of the

7

methods to be applied can do this. Finally, action must be taken to implement the plan that best reduces the production of wastes and pollutants. Throughout this three-step process, the government can act definitively and reliably as an enabling partner in fostering pollution prevention.

Additionally, pollution prevention involves multi-media approaches that work to solve environmental problems holistically rather than focusing on pollution in a single medium such as air, land, or water. Rules, regulations and solutions that are not multi-media may make existing problems worse. Sometimes this can result in the shifting of pollution from one medium to another. For example, in some cases, by requiring hazardous air emission controls for industrial facilities, other problems might result, such as pollutants being transferred to underground drinking water through the residual sludge. Pollution prevention activities ensure the minimization and elimination of wastes, and not the shifting of these wastes from one medium to another.

Opportunities

Pollution prevention 's effectiveness lies in the fact that it is a holistic, multi-media approach, with practical tools, such as Environmental Management Systems (EMS), environmentally preferable purchasing, multi-media inspections, and materials accounting practices that can be tailored to any industrial or community sector. The wide-ranging pollution prevention tool kit has the potential to tackle the daunting environmental challenges such as energy and water shortages, global climate change and chemical safety issues. Pollution Prevention is the only mechanism to provide concrete steps and identify quantifiable targets for better implementation of sustainable development.[12]

The proactive use of pollution prevention can decrease the strains on natural resources in environmental justice communities. Additionally, pollution prevention can help improve public health since disease often impacts most heavily on people with weak or compromised immune systems. Immune system damage often results from polluted water and pesticide use on chemical-intensive agricultural lands as well as consumption of crops grown on these lands. Proactive steps to use better technologies and less-toxic chemicals can likely improve local environmental quality, inequality, and poverty. Pollution prevention could even provide opportunities for job creation, capacity building and local empowerment in environmental justice communities.

BACKGROUND ON ENVIRONMENTAL JUSTICE

---

[12] Blueprint for Pollution Prevention and Sustainable Development, National Pollution Prevention Roundtable, August, 2002.

EPA defines environmental justice to mean the fair treatment of people of all races, cultures and incomes with respect to the development, implementation and enforcement of environmental laws and policies and their meaningful involvement in the decision-making processes of the government.[13] Communities of color and low-income communities have a long history of involvement in environmental quality issues.[14] Since the 1980's community organizations have been forming at the grass roots level to work more intensively on environmental pollution issues.[15] Recent concerns about environmental justice can be traced to public and private regional and national studies highlighting observational and statistical data indicating that low-income communities and communities of color are more likely than the general population to be exposed to pollution and to suffer from associated health effects due to exposure.[16]

In 1990 the University of Michigan held a conference on Race and the Incidence of Environmental Hazards.[17] Participants at that conference wrote to the Administrator of the Environmental Protection Agency seeking a meeting and action on a variety of issues relating to environmental risk in low-income communities and communities of color.[18] Former EPA Administrator William Reilly responded to that letter by forming the Environmental Equity Workgroup to examine issues of disproportionate risk in low-income communities and communities of color and to review agency programs and procedures in order to assure that EPA was fulfilling its mission with respect to those communities.[19] In response to public concerns, in 1992 the EPA also created an Office of Environmental Equity to facilitate the integration of environmental justice into EPA programs, policies and activities.

In 1993, Former EPA Administrator Carol Browner made environmental justice a priority stating "EPA is committed to addressing these concerns and assuming a leadership role in environmental justice to enhance environmental quality for all residents of the United States." In 1994, President William Clinton issued Executive Order 12898 to establish environmental justice as a national priority and to focus the attention of federal agencies on environmental and health conditions in low-income communities and communities of color with a view towards achieving environmental protection for all communities.

---

[13] Christine Todd Whitman, Environmental Protection Agency, EPA's Commitment to Environmental Justice, Memorandum, August 9, 2001.

[14] See Lawrence v. Hancock, 76 F. Supp. 1004, 1008 (S.D. W. Va. 1948); Simkins v. City of Greenboro, 149 F. Supp. 562 (M.D. N. C. 1957); Bohler v. Lane, 204 F. Supp. 168 (S.D. Fla. 1962); Beal v. Lindsay, 468 F. 2nd. 287 (2nd Cir. 1972).

[15] Bean v. Southwestern Management Corporation, 482 F. Supp 673 (1979; New York City Coalition to End Lead Poisoning v. Koch, 138 Misc. 2d 188 (1987); East-Bibb Twiggs Neighborhood Association et al. v. Macon-Bibb Planning and Zoning Commission et al., 662 F2d 1465 (1987); El Pueblo Para el Aire y Agua Limpio v. County of Kings, 22 ELR 20357 (1991).

[16] United Church of Christ, Commission for Racial Justice, Toxic Waste and Race in the United States: A National Report on the Racial and Socio-Economic Characteristics of Communities with Hazardous Waste Sites (1987).

[17] U.S. Environmental Protection Agency, Environmental Equity: Reducing Risks for all Communities, Volume 1 (1992).

[18] Id.

[19] Id.

As previously stated, Administrator Christine Todd Whitman confirmed [20] EPA's commitment to environmental justice, saying "[e]nvironmental justice is the goal to be achieved for all communities and persons across this nation" and that it will be achieved when everyone enjoys the same degree of protection from environmental and health hazards and has a "healthy environment where they live, learn and work." According to Administrator Whitman, achieving environmental justice is an objective imbedded in the federal environmental statutes. "Environmental statutes provide many opportunities to address environmental risks and hazards in minority and/or low income communities. Application of these existing statutory provisions is an important part of this Agency's effort to prevent those communities from being subject to disproportionately high and adverse impacts, and environmental effects."[21] Because it proactively seeks to integrate environmental justice in the Agency's mission as part of the application of existing statutory authorities, Administrator Whitman's 2001 memo represents a significant advance to the commitment to environmental justice made by previous administrations.

The leadership displayed by the EPA has been important to and supportive of the grass roots environmental justice movement that has always made the 'concept' of pollution prevention a guiding principle. The thread throughout the Principles of Environmental Justice, drafted at the First National People of Color Environmental Leadership Summit in 1991, is a call for pollution prevention.[22] The third principle calls for "ethical, balanced and responsible uses of land and renewable resources in the interest of a sustainable planet for humans and other living things".[23] Principle 6 demands the "cessation of the production of all toxins, hazardous wastes, and radioactive materials ...".[24]

---

[20] Christine Todd Whitman, Environmental Protection Agency, EPA's Commitment to Environmental Justice, Memorandum, August 9, 2001.
[21] Id.
[22] Center for Public Environmental Oversight, The First People of Color Environmental Leadership Summit, Principle of Environmental Justice (adopted: October 27, 1991) available at http://www.cpeo.org/pubs/ejprinc.html
[23] Id.
[24] Id.

POLLUTION PREVENTION AND ENVIRONMENTAL JUSTICE

Pollution prevention, as a concept, was identified at the First People of Color Environmental Leadership Summit as a policy necessary for achieving environmental justice because of the clear need to reduce pollution impacts and the broad range of damaging effects believed to result from pollution exposures. Even though communities may sometimes view pollution prevention, as defined by government, with skepticism, pollution prevention can have positive impacts on environmental justice communities by reducing pollution exposures and thereby improving quality of life.

The development and implementation of a multi-stakeholder collaborative model, increasing community and tribal capacity to participate in pollution prevention partnerships, and implementing opportunities to advance environmental justice through pollution prevention in federal environmental statutes are some of the major recommendations that have received endorsement from all the stakeholder groups as ways to effectively achieve these goals. Areas such as multi-media, multi-hazard reduction, waste minimization and product / process substitution have already demonstrated reductions in hazardous chemicals and solvents, achieved water and energy savings, and reduced carbon dioxide emissions. There are promising efforts in the area of transportation, alternative fuels, and small businesses in environmental justice communities.

The goals of pollution prevention, source reduction and protection of natural resources, have the potential to offer a variety of benefits to low-income, minority and tribal communities and would seem to be a natural coupling with environmental justice. Pollution prevention can reduce permitted and fugitive emissions and also accidental releases or spills and their attendant adverse health impacts. In addition to addressing regulated discharges, pollution prevention activities can go beyond existing environmental statutes and regulations.

The environmental justice movement is not only committed to the goals and values of pollution prevention, it actively seeks eliminated or reduced pollution, eliminated or reduced adverse health effects and improved environmental quality for low-income, minority and tribal communities—results that pollution prevention could produce. The concept of using pollution prevention as an environmental justice tool would seem to make perfect sense, but, for a number of reasons, community organizations have not, as a rule, added it to their environmental justice toolbox. Issues such as lack of capacity, lack of trust and failure to develop or include communities in collaborative models or partnerships have presented barriers to wider acceptance of the utility of pollution prevention in low-income communities and communities of color. Environmental justice requires that communities have more than an indirect influence on industry's production process when pollution prevention activities can lead to reduced pollution exposures, holistic community development and economic sustainability. This influence will benefit environmental justice communities for years to come.

For communities to have a direct influence on preventing, minimizing or eliminating pollution, capacity building in communities must be a priority of government and other stakeholders. This means communities need a basic understanding of pollution prevention processes and technologies, by industry or substantive areas, and of the steps needed to develop a collaborative model in which other stakeholders work with communities to implement process or technology changes.

ENFORCEMENT AND POLLUTION PREVENTION

It is important to understand the relationship between enforcement and pollution prevention as discussed in this report. All stakeholders agree that pollution prevention constitutes progress beyond the protection of human health and the environment mandated by compliance with all applicable regulatory standards. Pollution prevention is not a substitute for compliance. Indeed, a pollution prevention strategy improves environmental quality only if it is coupled with a vigorous enforcement program.

Effective enforcement is the foundation for pollution prevention progress for several reasons:

- First, enforcement assures that all facilities comply with regulatory obligations, thus incurring regulatory costs. The substantial cost of managing toxic materials and wastes in compliance with regulatory standards creates an important economic incentive to find savings through product substitution and other pollution prevention innovations. This economic incentive is vital because of the limited resources available to "reward" those who choose to go "beyond compliance."

- Second, enforcement is fundamental to gain community support for pollution prevention projects. The evidence of regulatory compliance in a strong enforcement program lends credulity to the regulated facilities themselves. Having demonstrated ability to comply with regulatory obligations, a facility earns the community's trust that it has the competence and responsibility to be recognized for the less-easily-monitored activities that frequently constitute pollution prevention.

- Third, enforcement sustains a level playing field of environmental costs among regulated entities. Without this baseline, one company cannot take the financial risk in an attempt to distinguish itself by going "beyond compliance." In a competitive market, one player cannot exceed by a large and unpredictable margin the environmental costs of its competitors. If it chooses to implement pollution prevention options other than those that are likely to produce cost savings, it will simply price itself out of business.

- Fourth, effective enforcement will help to ensure a level playing field for all companies. Enforcement provides the economic disincentive to violating regulatory requirements, while at the same time ensuring that companies in compliance will be able to benefit from the public good will that pollution prevention efforts usually bring. Enforcement is the "stick" counterpart to the economic "carrot" represented by pollution prevention. In that sense, strong enforcement plays an important complementary role to pollution prevention efforts.

Thus, rigorous enforcement is the companion of pollution prevention. Complexities emerge when this principle is applied at the facility and sector level. Smaller, less sophisticated firms often have difficulty understanding their permitting obligations and conforming to them. For large firms, the dynamic between pollution prevention and compliance is relatively simple: pollution prevention projects cannot be used to evade meeting the environmental performance mandated by applicable regulatory standards. Pollution prevention means exceeding an established standard, reducing an organization's environmental footprint in a manner not required by regulators, or improving environmental performance by reducing unregulated sources of emissions. A company subject to enforcement action for an instance of non-compliance does not forfeit the opportunity to engage in pollution prevention activities (which, after all, by definition reduce ambient pollution); but at the same time its participation in pollution prevention activities does not bar appropriate penalties for non-compliance.

For small businesses with challenges in understanding and achieving compliance, enforcement may need to be coupled with compliance assistance tools such as education and training before pollution prevention opportunities emerge. A more flexible approach may be required to achieve pollution reductions with sectors struggling to achieve baseline compliance. For currently unregulated sources (those not subject to permit requirements or other specific regulatory obligations), any voluntary step to reduce pollution could be termed pollution prevention. This designation of course goes away if the applicable regulatory authority creates mandatory compliance standards. In other words, pollution prevention is a rolling target, always exceeding the environmental standards promulgated as necessary to protect human health and the environment.

THE PRECAUTIONARY PRINCIPLE

Pollution prevention is consistent with the cautious approach to evaluating and addressing environmental risks that has been a cornerstone of many U.S. regulatory programs. Currently law and guidance are replete with examples of caution exercised in the face of scientific or technological uncertainty:

- The Clean Air Act's focus on health impacts without reference to cost
- New chemical review standards under the Toxic Substances Control Act
- The Food and Drug Administration's new drug approval process
- The Occupational Safety and Health Administration's implementation of the general duty clause

13

This report's recommendation to continue rigorous enforcement of regulatory standards while also stimulating use of pollution prevention that goes beyond compliance can be viewed in the light of this tradition of regulatory prudence.

This perspective does not conflict with the intent of the "precautionary principle" articulated in the 1992 Rio Declaration on Environment and Development, which stated that "[w]here there are threats of serious or irreversible damage, lack of scientific certainty shall not be used as a reason for postponing cost effective measures to prevent environmental degradation." There is scientific and government support in Europe for the Precautionary Principle theory; however, there has been some criticism that the implementation of the principle may generate litigation. Components of the "precautionary principle" support designing and implementing pollution prevention solutions. Pollution prevention provides an opportunity to act cautiously in the face of imperfect information, scientific uncertainty and high risk. From this perspective, pollution prevention presents an opportunity in environmental justice communities to enhance environmental quality in the face of multiple sources of pollution. To the extent that current regulatory standards may not have anticipated cumulative impacts or vulnerable populations, pollution prevention provides an opportunity to add a cautionary element of improved environmental protection.

TRIBAL GOVERNMENT AND POLLUTION PREVENTION

The concept of environmental justice can be difficult to apply to situations arising within Indian reservations. In most environmental justice cases, there are several kinds of entities involved, typically at least: a community comprised of minority and/or low-income people; a business that either wants to do or is doing something that causes environmental impacts that the community wants to prevent or stop; and a government agency that has permitting or other regulatory authority. Often there is more than one entity of one or another of these categories, for example, both a state and a federal agency, or more than one minority community that is up in arms.[25]

In Indian country, the tribe might fit into all three of these categories. The people who comprise the tribe might be seen as an environmental justice community, in that they are generally considered an ethnic minority (and perhaps a racial minority) and most of the families may also be low-income. The tribe is, of course, also a sovereign government, and as such may exercise regulatory or permitting authority over the facility that would

---

[25] Dean B. Suagee, *Dimensions of Environmental Justice in Indian Country and Native Alaska*, a policy paper prepared for the Second National People of Color Environmental Leadership Summit (Summit II), October 23-26, 2002, Washington, D.C. The Summit II policy papers are available on the web site of Clark Atlanta University, Environmental Justice Resource Center, at: www.ejrc.cau.edu, more specifically: www.ejrc.cau.edu/summitIIPolicyPapersTOC/html; David H. Getches and David N. Pellow, *Beyond "Traditional" Environmental Justice, in* JUSTICE AND NATURAL RESOURCES: CONCEPTS, STRATEGIES, AND APPLICATIONS, at 3, 16-26 (Kathryn Mutz, *et al.* eds, Island Press 2002) (discussing the problem of defining environmental justice so broadly that it could include claims made by any community, and suggesting that, whatever criteria are used to make the concept narrow enough to be useful, Indian tribes should generally be considered as EJ communities).

14

cause (or is causing) the environmental impacts that the community wants to stop. It is likely that, in addition to the tribe, a federal government agency or two also has some authority over the facility, but the tribe's status as a sovereign government is always an important factor in dealing with polluting facilities within reservation boundaries.

So, the tribe is the environmental justice community and the tribe is also a government with some measure of authority over the facility. In addition, the tribe may also be the business that operates, or seeks to operate, the polluting facility. The tribe might do this through a tribal enterprise or through a joint venture with a private business. Sometimes the tribe's role as owner/operator may be through a governmental institution, for example a utilities department that operates facilities such as wastewater treatment plants and landfills.

In non-Indian America, governments may also be involved on both sides of the regulatory regime, that is, as regulators and as operators of regulated facilities. There are usually some pretty well established walls, though, between government agency as regulator and government agency as proponent or operator or funder of regulated facilities. In Indian country, the distinctions between tribe as regulator and operator of regulated facility are often less clearly drawn and may be hard to maintain. Tribes, after all, are generally rather small communities, and community leaders often wear more than one hat. Moreover, people who perform roles in the tribe as government generally also perform important roles in the tribe as a community.

UNDERSTANDING POLLUTION IMPACTS

Communities of color, low-income and tribal communities suffer from numerous adverse pollution impacts from non-sustainable environmental practices that could be reduced or eliminated through pollution prevention measures. These impacts include unfavorable health effects and adverse impacts which are environmental, societal, economic, and international. Reducing all of these adverse impacts from pollution is a key concern of communities that is also shared by the Environmental Protection Agency. The chief goals of the major environmental protection statutes administered by EPA are "protection of public health and the environment." EPA's Framework for Pollution Prevention acknowledges the relationship between preventing adverse health impacts and preventing pollution by stating that partnership with the public health community is a key objective in order to demonstrate that "pollution prevention is disease prevention."[26]

Health and Environmental Impacts

Pollution prevention measures can reduce poor air quality that is believed to contribute to illness and premature death in communities. Outdoor air pollution is responsible for

---

[26] EPA Pollution Prevention Policy Framework, Guiding Social Principles, www.epa.gov/p2/p2ppolicy/framework htm.

increased morbidity and mortality locally[27] and throughout the world[28]. Research supports the community's view that asthma and other respiratory diseases, cancer, birth defects, liver and kidney damage and premature death, are all attributable, at least in part, to air pollution exposures[29]. Air pollution exposures due to residence in exposure zones of hazardous and other waste sites have also been associated with statistically increased risks of birth defects, breast cancer, and leukemia and bladder cancer.[30]

---

[27] Daniel M. Steigman, Is it "urban" or "asthma?", The Lancet, July 1996, at 143-144 (documenting much higher asthma hospital admission rates in poor and minority communities than in other areas of Boston); R. Charon Gwynn and George D. Thurston, The Burden of Air Pollution: Impacts among Racial Minorities, Environmental Health Perspectives, Volume 109, Supplement 4, August 2001 (exploring disparities in hospital admissions and mortality by race in New York City); Susan M. Bernard, Johnathan M. Samet, Anne Grambsch, Kristie L. Ebi, and Isabelle Romieu, The Potential Impacts of Climate Variability and Change on Air Pollution-Related Health Effects in the United States, Environmental Health Perspectives, Volume 109, Supplement 2, May 2001 (stating that air pollution can cause, respiratory diseases, cardiovascular diseases, alter host defenses, damage lung tissue, lead to premature death and contribute to cancer).

[28] Tom Bellander, Public Health and Air Pollution, The Lancet, January 2001, at 69-70 (estimating the increase of mortality as a result of long term studies of air pollution in Austria, France and Switzerland). Kunzli, N; Kaiser, R; Medina, S; Studnika, M; Chanel, O; Filliger, P; Herry, M; Horak, Jr. F; Puybonnieux-Texier,V; Quenel, P; Schneieder, J; Seethaler, R; Vergnaud, J-C; Sommer, H., Public Health Impact of Outdoor and Traffic Related Air Pollution: A European Assessment, The Lancet, September 2000, at 795-801 (finding that air pollution caused 6% more total mortality, 25,000 new cases of chronic bronchitis in adults, 290,000 additional cases of bronchitis in children, 500,000 more asthma attacks and 16 million person days of restricted activities); Jun Kagawa, Atmospheric Air Pollution Due to Mobile Sources and Effects on Human Health in Japan, Environmental Health Perspectives 102, Supplement 4, October 1994 (finding that unfavorable human health effects result from automobile caused air pollution in large cities and along transportation routes); Tony Sheldon, Reducing Greenhouse Gases Will Have Good Short Tern Effect, British Medical Journal, Volume 321, page 1367, December 2002 (finding that bronchitis in children fell ten percent in relation to reduced concentrations of particulate matter).

[29] Tracey J. Woodruff, Daniel Axelrad, Jane Caldwell, Rachel Morello-Frosch, and Arlene Rosenbaum, Public Health Implications of 1990 Air Toxics Concentrations across the United States, Environmental Health Perspectives, Volume 106, May 1998; Rachel A. Morello-Frosch, Tracey J. Woodruff, Daniel A. Axelrad, Jane C. Caldwell, Air Toxics and Health Risks in California: The Public Health Implications of Outdoor Concentrations, Risk Analysis, Volume 20 Issue 2, February 2000 (predicting 8600 excess cancer cases and for non-cancer health effects a median total hazard index of 17). A national study of air toxics data found that 10% of all census tracts had one or more carcinogenic hazardous air pollutants present in excess of the defined health benchmark concentrations for cancer and non-cancer health effects and over 90% of census tracts had estimated concentrations of benzene, formaldehyde and 1-3 butadiene greater than the cancer health benchmark.

[30] Sandra Geschwind, Jan Stolwijk, Micheal Bracken, Edward Fitzgerald, Alice Stark, Carolyn Olsen, and James Melius, Risk of Congenital Malformations Associated with Proximity to Hazardous Waste Sites, American Journal of Epidemiology, Volume 136, No. 11, 1992 (finding an additional risk of bearing children with birth defects associated with residence near hazardous waste sites); Samuel S. Epstein, Environmental and Occupational Pollutants are Avoidable Causes of Breast Cancer, 24 Int'. J. Health Servs., 145,147, 1994; Elizabeth L. Lewis-Michl, Ph.D., R. Kallenbach, Ph.D., Nannette S. Geary, James M. Melius, M.D., Dr. P.H., Carole L. Ju, M.S.,Maureen F. Orr, M.S., Steven P. Forand, Investigation of Cancer Incidence and Residence Near 38 Landfills with Soil Migration Conditions: New York State 1980-1989 (showing statistically significantly elevated risks for female bladder cancer and female leukemia among women residing in the landfill exposure buffers).

Pollution prevention can also reduce the risk of cancer and non-cancer health effects in the occupational context for workers who are typically the first to be subjected to environmental exposures. However, improperly designed pollution prevention activities may increase workers' environmental burdens. For example, water based paints reduce VOCs released to the environment, but the strong non-oxidizing biocides required for bacterial control pose a greater risk to the worker.

Pollution prevention can also reduce the devastating effects of pollution on the environment for plants, animals, marine life and other living things including people who rely on the environment for subsistence food gathering. Some pollutants are persistent (degrade slowly) and bioaccumulate in the environment, often becoming part of the food chain ultimately consumed by people. These types of pollutants, persistent bioaccumulative toxics, are commonly referred to as PBT's. Health effects from subsistence food consumption can translate into extraordinarily high risks for cancer and non-cancer health effects[31].

Native American and Alaskan Native Nations can benefit from pollution prevention because they are exposed to many of the same environment threats as other communities of color. They suffer from adverse effects of pesticides and other hazardous substances.[32] These exposures result into a variety of adverse health effects including asthma, hypertension, thyroid disorders, cancer and leukemia. Pollution has also impacted upon their ability to engage in traditional cultural practices.[33]

Risks to Native Nations have not historically been adequately addressed due to erratic levels of federal technical and financial assistance, particularly in cases where the funding mechanism failed to recognize the appropriate role of tribal governments. [34] All activities that impact upon tribal resources should be revisited to determine whether and

---

[31] According to the NEJAC Fish Consumption Report, low-income communities, communities of color and tribes have subsistence fish consumption rates ranging from the 90th to the 99th percentile rates for the general population. These fish consumption rates translate into extraordinarily high risks for cancer and non-cancer health effects;Industrial Technology Associates, EPA Cumulative Exposure Assessment for Greenpoint-Williamsburg, 2000 (concluding that total cancer risks from fish consumption range from 1 in 10 to 1 in 1000); Jason Corburn, Combining Community-Based Research and Local Knowledge to Confront Asthma and Subsistence Fishing Hazards in Greenpoint-Williamsburg, Brooklyn, New York, Environmental Health Perspectives Supplements, Volume 110, Number 2, April 2002.

[32] Lorraine Halinka Malcoe, Robert A. Lynch, Michelle Cozier Kegler and Valrie A. Skaggs, Lead Sources, Behaviors and Socioeconomic Factors in Relation to Blood Lead of Native American and White Children, Environmental Health Perspectives Supplements, Volume 110, Number 2, April 2002; Somini Sengupta, A Sick Tribe and a Dump as a Neighbor, The New York Times, April 7, 2001.

[33] U.S. Fish and Wildlife Service, Division of Environmental Quality, Pesticides and Wildlife, Pesticides and Wildlife, July 2001, http://contaminants.fws.gov/Issues/Pesticides.cfm.; Lisa Mastny, Coming to Terms with the Artic, Worldwatch Institute, Worldwatch, Volume 13, p. 24, January 2000.

[34] Mary Arquette, Maxine Cole, Katsi Cook, Brenda LaFrance, Margaret Peters, James Ransom, Elvera Sargent, Vivian Smoke and Arlene Stairs, Holistic Risk-Based Environmental Decision Making: A Native Perspective, Environmental Health Perspectives Supplements, Volume 110, Number 2, April 2002

how pollution prevention measures can benefit tribes.[35] As sovereign governments, tribes can play a vital role in pollution prevention and help eliminate the risks associated with the release of pollution into the environment. Tribes can mitigate the impacts of shifting pollution from one medium to another while protecting natural resources for future tribal generations.

Societal and Developmental Impacts

Societal and developmental impacts believed by communities to be pollution related can be reduced through pollution prevention. Disparities in socioeconomic status result in health disparities that are exacerbated by environmental exposures.[36] Health care opportunities, health status, educational opportunities, intergenerational transfers of wealth, poverty and lack of health insurance are all measures of socioeconomic status that increase the risk of health disparities and are effected by both race and pollution exposures.[37]

The reduction or elimination of pollution, especially PBTs, would be an effective way to address developmental damage and delay that is more likely to occur when children are exposed to multiple and cumulative risks in their environment.[38] Certain pollutants also have adverse impacts on the reproductive system, and a special concern is endocrine disruptors since they are extremely persistent, bioaccumulate, and therefore have a multi-generational impact. Numerous pollutants targeted for toxic pollution reduction activities, including lead, mercury and polychlorinated biphenyls, are neurodevelopment toxicants and cause learning disabilities, attention deficit hyperactivity disorder, developmental delays and emotional and behavioral problems.[39]

Although the impacts on human health in tribal communities may be similar to impacts suffered by other environmental justice communities, tribal communities may also suffer impacts on cultural practices that are unique to them. The inability to carry on traditional cultural practices such as consumption of wild foods or the use of plant materials in crafts might seriously impair the ability of the elders of a tribe to pass on traditions to younger tribal members. This is a kind of disproportionate impact that is largely unique to tribal communities.

---

[35] U.S. Environmental Protection Agency, National Tribal Council and Tulalip Tribes, Pollution Prevention and Native American Communities: A Tool for Tribal Environmental Protection and Impact Assessment, supra at p. 10.

[36] Nancy E. Alder, and Katherine Newman, Socioeconomic Disparities in Health: Pathways and Policies: Inequality in Education, Income and Occupation Exacerbates the Gaps Between the "Haves" and the "Have-nots", Health Affairs, April 2002

[37] Id.

[38] Francine Clark Jones, Community Violence, Children and Youth: Considerations For Program, Policy and Nursing Roles, Pediatric Nursing, Volume 23, p. 131, March 1997.

[39] Ted Schettler, Toxic Threats to Neurological Development of Children, Environmental Health Perspectives, Volume 109, Supplement 6, December 2001

Economic Impacts

Communities believe that pollution prevention would be a proactive way to address the adverse economic impacts of pollution that exacerbate poverty and reduce earning ability. Pollution exposure has adverse economic impact on the cost of access to health care in environmental justice communities. Pollution exposures place a huge economic burden on society. Just four diseases associated with environmental causation cost the United States and Canada as much as 397 billion dollars a year.[40] There is emerging evidence of economic impacts associated with reduced intelligence from pollution exposures. Pollution also jeopardizes property values in impacted communities. Decreased property values translate into loss of equity for use in getting bank loans, and makes it more difficult to sell the property and relocate. Economic data indicates that residence near the fence line of industrial facilities has an adverse economic effect on property values whether or not the property is actually contaminated.[41] Property that is actually contaminated by a nearby source or with contaminated drinking water may be essentially worthless.

Communities inundated with brownfields, Superfund sites, and other abandoned, contaminated lands suffer adverse economic impacts and continuing health risks. Though some funding opportunities exist via new initiatives for brownfields redevelopment, funding is limited. Despite the Superfund and Brownfields programs, many contaminated sites have yet to be addressed.

In communities and indigenous lands throughout the country, subsistence farmers and fisherman depend on the land to provide food for their families. Pollutants, especially PBTs and heavy metals that enter the food chain can devastate this way of life. In addition, those small community businesses such as fish farms that depend on the environmental health of the water and land are also economically harmed.

In urban centers, abandoned properties create blight, accelerating the economic decline of the surrounding area. Rural communities may suffer similar harms when large tracts of land become contaminated and are then abandoned.

International Impacts

Pollution prevention has the potential to reduce pollution impacts on an international level. Globalization has resulted in the shifting of industrial production to developing

---

[40] Tom Muir and Mike Zegarac, Societal Costs of Exposure to Toxic Substances, Environmental Health Perspectives, Volume 109, Supplement 6, December 2001.
[41] Paul S. Kibel, FAB Quarterly Viewpoint, Full Cleanup Preserves Full Value, www.fablae.com/cleanup htm.; Mundy Associates, LLC, Contaminated Property: Issues and Answers, June 2002, www.mundyassoc.com/contaminated.htm.

countries along with accompanying pollution and adverse health-related effects.[42] Global warming due to fossil fuel use, increased use of pesticides, and exploitation of natural resources in Third World countries cause loss of biodiversity, erosion and deforestation. Unsustainable policies and practices could be reduced through pollution prevention measures.[43] Most developing countries also do not have effective environmental regulation. History shows that lack of environmental regulation enables industries that produce toxic waste to be less vigorous in preventing pollution.

Pollution prevention is, at heart, a highly ethical concept that is wholly consistent with notions of environmental justice. That is why reduction of the use of non-renewable resources was identified at the First People of Color Environmental Leadership Summit as the 17th Principles of Environmental Justice—"using as little as possible of Mother Earth's resources." This principle is about sustainable development and fairness to subsequent generations. International efforts to promote sustainable development have resolved that issue and adopted the concept of "intergenerational equity" as a way to consider human impacts on the environment through the prism of time and fairness. Intergenerational equity is said to have three components: conservation of options for future generations --the diversity of the resource base should be conserved so as to allow future generations to have the freedom to make their own choices; conservation of quality --the environment should be passed on to the next generation in the same condition as when the present generation received it; and conservation of access -- all members of the present generation should have equitable access to natural resources.[44] Intergenerational equity requires that we conserve existing natural resources so that coming generations have the resources needed to sustain healthy and productive lives. The focus of pollution prevention on source reduction is consistent with moral obligations in favor of subsequent generations of people and other living things.

Using pollution prevention approaches to advance environmental justice is also supportive of and synergistic with EPA's philosophy of pollution prevention. Issues such as climate change, that have far reaching national and international ramifications for recent and future generations, reduction of smog, and energy efficiency improvements are already part of EPA's programs and policies. Similarly, loss of biodiversity through habitat loss and alteration and associated impacts on future generations are a concern of EPA's Brownfields Revitalization Program, a program that strives to assure that greenfields are protected and urban land is redeveloped in sustainable ways.

---

[42] Khabir Ahmed, World Bank Predicts Development for the Next Century, The Lancet, September 18, 1999; Indoor Air Pollution Exposure Well Over WHO Guidelines, Health & Medicine Week, October 2-October 9, 2000; Kenny Pronezuk, James Akre, Gerald Moy, Constanza Vallenas, Global Perspectives in Breast Milk Contamination: Infectious and Toxic Hazards, Environmental Health Perspectives, Volume 110, Number 6, June 2002.

[43] Joy Chen, Rachel Rivera, A Pocket Guide to the Environmental Millennium, The Amicus Journal, Volume 21, p. 22, January 2000; Richard Fenske, Incorporating Health and Ecological Costs into Agricultural Production, Environmental Health Perspectives, Volume 110, Number 5, May 2002.

[44] Duncan French, Sustainable Development and the 1991 Madrid Protocol to the 1959 Antarctic Treaty: The Primacy of Protection in a Particularly Sensitive Environment, Journal of International Wildlife Law & Policy, Section No. 3, Vol. 2; Pg. 291,September 22, 1999.

Pollution prevention can help us meet environmental challenges faced by the human family. In the words of Administrator Whitman, "[b]ecause we have been entrusted with the stewardship of this shared planet, we must all work together. By drawing on the strengths of others—and by willingly sharing our own—we can fulfill our sacred obligation to future generations to leave them a cleaner planet than we found."

TOWARD A MULTI-STAKEHOLDER COLLABORATIVE MODEL TO ADVANCE ENVIRONMENTAL JUSTICE THROUGH POLLUTION PREVENTION: *Addressing Environmental Quality and Economic Justice Issues through Multi-stakeholder Pollution Prevention Collaborations*

Introduction

Collaborative approaches to improving environmental quality through pollution prevention have utilized a variety of approaches aimed at reducing or preventing pollution and promoting a more sustainable economy. The Environmental Protection Agency's Common Sense Initiative and Project Excel are two of many examples of successful pollution prevention collaborations. However, community-driven pollution prevention collaborative models have been the exception rather than the rule, and community driven collaborative models have lacked a formal structure.

Efforts to use collaborative processes have not always included tribal communities in appropriate ways. Tribes as governments may have regulatory authority over some aspect of a problem. Tribes may need to be included in collaboration because they have rights under treaties or statutes outside their territorial jurisdiction. The people who comprise a tribe, or a group within the tribe, may be a community with environmental justice concerns that should be included as stakeholders. In the discussion of collaborative models in this section, the implications for tribal communities have not always been elaborated. Readers may want to supply their own expansion on the text presented.

Currently, no uniform model exists for a community-driven multi-stakeholder, pollution prevention collaborative. A community-driven multi-stakeholder model would feature the common goal of a healthy local environment and highlight the need to share responsibility for achieving that goal. A community-driven model would take a broad look at environmental concerns in the community, identify the most effective ways to improve health, and utilize the potential of collaboration and mobilizing local resources to make progress in improving the health status of local residents. A community-driven collaborative model would acknowledge the importance of sharing information and establishing a level playing field for all participants. This kind of collaborative model can help build sustainable community capacity to understand and improve the environment. (Details on the structure and action plans towards a collaborative model are described in recommendation #1.)

A community-driven multi-stakeholder pollution prevention collaborative model would need to involve all major stakeholders as equals and incorporate sustainable economic development with a focus on improving the quality of life and health of community members. The model would be a means of addressing environmental quality and economic justice issues through community-driven multi-stakeholder pollution prevention collaborations.

Initial Scoping Meetings: Drafting the Petition

A community driven multi-stakeholder pollution prevention collaboration would begin with initial scoping meetings during which the impacted community would get together as a group and identify their issues and basic concerns in general terms. The universe of their issues or a specific issue could be the focus of the discussion. The issues would be discussed orally and issues articulated in a draft Environmental Justice Petition that would ultimately be presented to a regulatory agency.

The initial scoping meetings would only involve the community and its technical assistants. Communities routinely have their concerns dismissed and need to be assured that their instincts can be trusted. The community would need to work with an organizer, advocate, technical and/or legal support personnel to preliminarily investigate the issues identified using available data and information on line. The community concerns and identified issues should be validated and confirmed for the community using preliminarily available information in an initial training/capacity building meeting.

Building the Collaboration

After the initial scoping and submission of petition meeting, an entity or organization would help the community organize the initial multi-stakeholder meeting. Working with its technical support or organizers, the community needs to identify all stakeholders pertinent to addressing the issues and concerns raised regarding pollution reduction. The stakeholders should include industry, small business, municipal government, state, tribal and local environmental regulatory agencies, state, tribal and local health agencies, elected representatives and emergency responders. Other key stakeholders include Chambers of Commerce, health organizations, civic organizations, environmental organizations, as appropriate, and technical assistance organizations, as appropriate. All stakeholders must be invited to join the collaboration. Reluctant or missing stakeholders should be strongly urged to participate.

Organizing the Initial Collaboration Meeting

At the initial collaboration meeting, all stakeholders should identify who they are, what they do and what their interests are. This will enable all participants to understand what the perspectives and expectations are for participating members. The stakeholders should brainstorm to identify their needs and what their anticipated benefits will be.

At this juncture, the community draft environmental justice petition should be shared with the other stakeholders. In small breakout groups, information and capacity building needs for each stakeholder should be identified, articulated and documented.

At a minimum, government agencies need a training and information package on how this collaboration will improve the process and develop trust within the community. Government needs to know what benefits it can anticipate from this process. A major function of government in a multi-stakeholder pollution prevention collaboration is education. Government needs education on how it can more effectively carry out its role and provide technical assistance. Government needs to commit resources, including an identified staff person to participate. Government also needs to commit staff persons or consultants who can serve as technical assistance providers to identify appropriate and available specific pollution prevention approaches designed to address the concerns raised. A facilitator may be employed to assist in developing a consensus process. Finally, an independent observer can assist by documenting the process and measuring pollution reductions achieved.

The needs of industry must also be met in order for industry and small business to successfully participate in this process. At a minimum, industry needs an information package on how they can benefit from the process, including how pollution prevention can improve profitability. Industry can benefit from compliance assistance centers developed with the support of government, training on the collaborative process and how it works, and help from a technical assistance provider to identify appropriate and available specific pollution prevention approaches designed to address the concerns raised.

A priority should be placed upon meeting the educational, training, capacity building and informational needs of the community. The community needs include, at a minimum, education pertaining to the environmental and health concerns raised, the regulatory provisions addressing pollution as it pertains to those concerns, and the role of pollution in affecting local health and environmental quality. A technical assistance provider and /or organizer is essential to helping the community participate on a level playing field with other stakeholders. It may be necessary to simplify materials or present them in language that lay persons can easily understand. Language appropriate training or educational materials may also be needed if English is not the language spoken by the community. A suitable regular meeting space is necessary, and the community may need assistance with communication materials and strategies. Community members also require financial support to participate in a community-driven collaborative. This support should include, at a minimum, resources and/or stipends, publication costs and transportation assistance.

In order to assure the success of the initial collaboration meeting, governmental and business stakeholders should identify information to be made available to the community relevant to their issues and basic concerns. Identified information should be shared through an information exchange arranged to take place before the next multi-stakeholder collaborative meeting.

Community Training: Refining the Issues and Setting Goals

Involvement of a non-stakeholder expert or organizing entity in both partnership building and the relevant subject area is crucial to the success of multi-stakeholder dialogues. This partnership builder or organizing entity would help to catalyze community-based action by researching the local concerns, identifying and engaging the stakeholders, adapting the EPA methodology and dialogue model to the community concern in question, facilitating the initial discussion between stakeholders and establishing systems for ongoing community-based action to resolve the concern. With assistance from the organizing entity, community organizers or technical assistance providers, the information exchanged is thoroughly reviewed by technical and legal advisors.

The community training/educational session should be based upon identified issues and information exchanged. The summary of this information should be fully developed. If needed, materials in appropriate language should be developed at this juncture to assist in the training.

The identified issues should be assessed, prioritized and refined by the community. The assessments should include discussion of the magnitude of the issues, the severity of the problem including the number of people impacted and whether a susceptible population is involved, the type of impact, whether there are also natural resources impacts and issues that present the greatest opportunities for improvement. The rationale for prioritization should consider these assessment factors. The assessment should produce a consensus with identifiable, articulated goals, recommendations and an action plan. The action plan should also contain metrics, such as identified goals, and expected compliance dates and evaluation dates.

The community training must prepare the community to participate on a level playing field including preparation respecting how to present their issues. This training and preparation should occur before the next multi-stakeholder collaborative meeting. At a minimum, at the community training the technical assistance provider should also provide information on how compliance can be achieved and on how pollution prevention measures, appropriate and specific to the prioritized issues, can be implemented.

Prior to the next multi-stakeholder meeting, government and industry or business should also undertake training of its stakeholder group in order to assure that all stakeholders understand the benefits of the process, their role and the need for commitment and participation of all stakeholders. Materials developed for each training should be shared and available for use if the project is replicated. Similarly, the proposed action plan should also be shared.[45]

Action Plan Developed through the Multi-stakeholder Process

The action plan should be memorialized in an enforceable agreement such as Memorandum of Agreements ("MOAs") or Good Neighbor Agreements, with identified demonstration projects and time frames for compliance. Good Neighbor Agreements between community groups and industrial companies have previously been developed in certain impacted communities to address acute and chronic environmental and economic problems. The Good Neighbor Agreements balance community sustainable development with the welfare of the community. Good neighbor agreements facilitate relationship building between the community and the industrial facility stakeholders.

Once there is consensus on identified priorities, the action plan and an agreement to memorialize it, the action should be commenced according to the proposed action plan. Targets for specific pollution reductions should be clear. Pollution reductions should be monitored on a regular basis by an independent consultant.

All subsequent multi-stakeholder meetings should include all stakeholders and there should be a process in place to assure that all stakeholders are invited. The community-driven multi-stakeholder collaboration process should also culminate in demonstration projects that can be implemented as identified in the action plan. These projects should be replicable projects that are consistent with and achieve identified goals. These projects should also include mechanisms to measure progress over time and assure that,

---

[45] A recent example of a collaborative partnership that demonstrated the need for community capacity-building can be found in the Common Sense Initiative ("CSI"), Printing Sector, New York City Education Project. [45] See U.S. Environmental Protection Agency, Environmental Compliance and Pollution Prevention, Technical Assistance Directory for Printers, New York City. P. 3 (referencing the New York City Education Project) (1998). This project challenged communities to identify community-based printers, to engage the printers about pollution prevention and to encourage them to undertake pollution prevention measures with technical assistance funded by EPA. When CSI community representatives indicated that EPA was looking at printers, community members asked what printers had done and why printers were being singled out. In order to educate the community groups that participated, a project specific Printing Sector Community Education Manual was developed that described the nature of the printing business including its size, the hazardous substances used in the printing industry, the health effects of the chemicals and products used in printing, alternatives processes and products available and the societal and economic benefits of using more sustainable processes and products.

Once prepared with an adequate background on the need for their local printers to undertake pollution prevention measures, community organizations identified more than 120 printers located in impacted communities, including some operating outside of the regulatory framework, that were interested in receiving technical assistance for pollution prevention. The community groups provided these printers with Design for the Environment and other pollution prevention materials for printers that demonstrated opportunities to prevent, minimize or eliminate pollution impacts. After receiving training in pollution prevention opportunities for printers, community groups, as their customers, were successful in encouraging local printers, to be good neighbors and engage in pollution prevention measures that would benefit their employees, their bottom line and the entire neighborhood.

25

at least on a quarterly basis, progress be evaluated. Once goals are met, it is important to set new goals.

In closing, community-driven multi-stakeholder collaborations already implemented using this model have produced win-win situations to industry, communities, and the government.

POLLUTION PREVENTION AND ENVIRONMENTAL JUSTICE FRAMEWORK

The NEJAC includes representatives from all stakeholder groups, reflects the views of key stakeholders and was convened to assure that diverse perspectives of those with an interest in environmental justice and pollution prevention would be heard and addressed. The workgroup members articulated their expectations from the process, identified areas of common ground and agreed to a framework for examining pollution prevention and environmental justice. The framework for examining the relationship between pollution prevention and environmental justice includes the following premises:

1. Pollution prevention activities should have a strong nexus with health, environmental and quality of life concerns of impacted communities and risk reduction and would benefit from process analysis for assessing which are the most important sources to focus attention on. For impacted communities, an extremely important value of pollution prevention is reducing health risks and improving quality of life. However some pollution impacts may be more easily addressed and others have the potential to achieve greater benefits by reducing toxicity or impacts to susceptible populations. In order to prioritize pollution prevention initiatives to provide the greatest benefit to environmental justice communities, those initiatives must address the most important sources to reduce risk, and improve health, environmental quality and quality of life.

2. Pollution prevention activities should recognize and respect the importance and value of community knowledge and experience and include the full participation of the impacted community. Communities possess information respecting community vulnerabilities, demographics and operational variation in local facilities and this information can improve prioritization in pollution prevention projects. Communities support the idea of pollution prevention but often lack specific information respecting the facilities susceptible to pollution prevention, the measures, strategies and technologies available to prevent or eliminate pollution and the substantive areas where pollution prevention can be useful. This means that efforts must be undertaken to build capacity within the community to enable the community to participate as full partners in efforts to prevent, minimize or eliminate pollution.

3. Pollution prevention activities should focus on all sources, including large and small facilities, public and private facilities, new and old facilities, and area and

ADVANCING ENVIRONMENTAL JUSTICE THROUGH POLLUTION PREVENTION
NEJAC Pollution Prevention Report
June 2003

mobile sources. Pollution prevention initiatives that will advance environmental justice must include a wide range of sources and activities. Focusing on stationary sources alone is inadequate to address the range of sources adversely impacting upon low-income communities and communities of color. At least fifty percent of the impacts of air pollution result from mobile sources. Pollution prevention initiatives for small facilities that are numerous such as dry cleaners, printers or auto body shops located in impacted communities may be just as important as reductions from individual stationary sources.

4. Pollution prevention should involve collaborations between all stakeholder groups and build capacity (through relevant tools, knowledge and education, and resources, where needed), should include adequate resources at the state and federal level and should promote new and emerging and existing technologies. Pollution prevention initiatives that promote environmental justice must include goal-oriented principled partnerships between all impacted stakeholders and capacity-building support where needed to enable low-income communities, communities of color and small businesses to participate on a level playing field, and must advance innovation as well as existing technologies to reduce pollution.

5. Pollution prevention should strive to be proactive, positive, solution-oriented, and holistic in approach (i.e., multi-media, in the context of sustainable and community development) and involve restoration, redevelopment and building sustainable economics through pollution prevention. Pollution prevention approaches that advance environmental justice should not be fragmented or demonstrate short-term vision. Traditional single media or media specific measures set forth in federal statutes and state delegated programs have limitations in that they often allow transfer of pollution from one media to another, focus on controlling large sources, ignoring other unregulated sources that may produce as much or more pollution and accept set amounts of pollution without incentives for regulated entities to go beyond compliance. Rather, successful approaches should consider long-term economic impacts on communities, workers and the environment.

6. Pollution prevention should involve culture change in institutions and management systems such as government, business, and schools and include accountability for measuring, monitoring, reviewing, evaluation and rewarding (where appropriate) performance. For pollution prevention to have a transformative impact on low-income communities and communities of color, it must permeate all levels of institutions including leadership in government, industry and educational and cultural institutions and reflect a change in how we approach the relationship between society and the environment. Policy pronouncements must lead to demonstrated and sustained commitments. Commitments should be encouraged with incentives and must be documented by measurable improvements. Successes should be noted and replicated.

7. Pollution prevention should apply relevant lessons from global experience. Successful international examples, especially in developing countries, of waste minimization, energy conservation and toxic use reduction can be incorporated into existing pollution prevention programs and policies. Similarly, there are examples in developing nations of more sustainable production practices that can be applied to situations in the United States.

8. Pollution prevention should promote the use of new and emerging technologies (i.e., alternative fuels, renewable energy, etc.). Opportunities currently exist to meet the needs of society using more sustainable technologies, products and processes. These new approaches are available to reduce pollution in some of the important areas for impacted communities including industrial production, land use and development, infrastructure development, public and private transportation and of the delivery of goods.

9. Pollution prevention should build on what exists. Federal environmental statutes, state, tribal and local statutes, programs, policies and initiatives currently exist to reduce, eliminate or prevent pollution. Tax subsidies, incentives, green purchasing programs, technical support projects and successful pilots currently exist to reduce pollution. Successful programs and initiatives should form the basis for integrating pollution prevention more fully into institutions and societal awareness.

10. Pollution prevention should address special economic, political, social, public health, and environmental attributes of at risk and/or underserved subpopulations (i.e., tribes, children, others, etc). A wealth of evidence indicates that not everyone is affected the same way by pollution exposures. The developing neonate, children, the elderly, people with compromised immune systems, individuals suffering from nutritional deficiencies or other health deficits and people with inadequate access to health care experience worse health outcomes at similar levels of exposure. Pollution prevention should be aggressively used to reduce pollution impacts on vulnerable populations. It offers an opportunity to target measures that can have the most benefit to susceptible groups in low-income communities and communities of color.

11. Pollution prevention activities should acknowledge and value the indispensable role of enforcement as a necessary complement, particularly in impacted communities. While pollution prevention activities are often defined as those that go beyond compliance, pollution prevention is never intended to preclude or serve as a substitute for environmental enforcement and compliance. Many impacted communities need traditional environmental enforcement mechanisms to be utilized to assure that compliance takes place. Blank]

Chapter 2: Consensus Recommendations

The National Environmental Justice Advisory Council (NEJAC) is making the following consensus recommendations to the U.S. Environmental Protection Agency (EPA) on advancing environmental justice through pollution prevention. In making these recommendations, the NEJAC urges that EPA implement these recommendations with the full participation of all appropriate stakeholder groups. These include impacted communities, government at all levels (federal, state, tribal, and local), business and industry, and others. Implementation of the recommendations will improve the quality of the environment for all people, in particular low-income, minority and tribal communities. However, without the active engagement of these communities, sustaining the benefits of these recommendations will be virtually impossible. An involved community has a vested interest in the process and this will enhance the chances for immediate and long-term success. Business and industry also benefit through reduced environmental impacts as these types of changes often lead to more efficient processes, save money, and create jobs. By truly involving other groups, government fulfill its promise as an instrument of empowerment. Therefore, the active participation of all groups is to everyone's benefit and key to the successful implementation of these recommendations.

There are 14 recommendations that have been grouped under three different categories: Community and Tribal involvement, Capacity Building, and Partnerships; More Effective Utilization of Tools and Programs; and Sustainable Processes and Products.

I. COMMUNITY AND TRIBAL INVOLVEMENT, CAPACITY BUILDING, AND PARTNERSHIPS

I-1. Develop and Promote Implementation of a Multi-stakeholder Collaborative Model to Advance Environmental Justice through Pollution Prevention that Ensures a Meaningful Role in Design and Implementation for Impacted Communities.

Background: Development of a multi-stakeholder collaborative model to advance environmental justice through pollution prevention is the recommendation that arguably has received the strongest endorsement from all stakeholder groups. This recommendation reflects the desire of impacted communities, tribes, business and industry, and government for support (programmatic, financial, technical) of community-driven and community-based processes in pollution prevention that clearly identify issues of concern, set measurable objectives, yield real environmental benefits, and offer meaningful opportunities for constructive engagement between the various stakeholders. A multi-stakeholder model is envisioned as a tool for communities, industry and government and should effectively gauge environmental impacts, implement pollution prevention technologies and assess the results from both a monetary and environmental standpoint.

ADVANCING ENVIRONMENTAL JUSTICE THROUGH POLLUTION PREVENTION
NEJAC Pollution Prevention Report
June 2003

From 1995 thru 2001, EPA supported a competitive grants program for Environmental Justice thru Pollution Prevention. The grants provided support for environmental justice communities and tribes to try innovative pollution prevention approaches to the environmental problems that they faced. While EPA no longer funds this program, there is precedent for EPA to provide funding for the types of activities encompassed in these recommendations. It is not essential for EPA to restore the earlier grants program, but it is essential to assure adequate funding and a competitive funding mechanism for the multi-stakeholder process discussed here, as well as the related recommendations in this report.

In putting forth this recommendation, the NEJAC is offering a set of guidelines to EPA regarding how to implement and achieve such collaborative efforts to advance environmental justice through pollution prevention. EPA should ensure the following:

- Secure adequate institutional, technical and financial resources.
- Provide assistance and facilitation to build the community's capacity to meaningfully provide direction to such efforts.
- Facilitate the development of multi-stakeholder partnerships.
- Identify clear pollution prevention opportunities and methods to achieve pollution prevention.
- Link pollution protection efforts to community based health concerns, lead testing and abatement, brownfields redevelopment and revitalization, transportation and air issues; local area multi-media hazards reduction, use of SEPs, promotion of clean energy, and others.
- Assist in developing, with the inclusion of a science based approach that includes traditional knowledge, measurable goals and clear environmental outcomes.
- Provide, where appropriate, use of consensus building (facilitation, mediation) and dispute resolution.

Action Items:

a. Develop a multi-stakeholder (communities, industry and government) collaborative model in order to reduce pollution in environmental justice communities. The content of this model is described in the consensus chapter. Successful pollution prevention methods and approaches already developed by EPA and other stakeholder groups should also be incorporated. A process should be developed to monitor and incorporate new and other sustainable development and pollution prevention initiatives. This model should be used by all the stakeholder groups for purposes that include:
    1. Capacity building for communities,
    2. Innovative technology transfer to industry,
    3. Leveraging of government programs.

b. Identify opportunities to integrate the use of the multi-stakeholder collaborative model to advance environmental justice though pollution prevention.

c. A program such as Performance Tracks Award, which provides an opportunity for community involvement to promote multi-stakeholder participation and pollution prevention, should be implemented and incorporated in the multi-stakeholder model. This award program should provide incentives not only to manufacturing facilities and small businesses, but also to the communities in the surrounding area.

d. Initiate a new Environmental Justice/Pollution Prevention Grants Program utilizing the multi-stakeholder collaborative model.

e. Build upon lessons learned from earlier programs and approaches relating to Environmental Justice and Pollution Prevention.

f. Build on successful programs, especially regional programs, and transfer those successes in implementation of similar programs in other parts of the country. For example, successful auto-refinishing programs were initiated in Oklahoma, South Carolina, Rhode Island, Massachusetts and Maryland, but the programs were developed in a vacuum and did not use other programs as resource. In addition, EPA's Design for Environment program has worked extensively in auto-refinishing and could provide additional material. The utilization of already developed materials should be used as criterion in the selection of grants.

I-2. Increase Community and Tribal Participation in Pollution Prevention Partnerships by Promoting Capacity-building for Pollution Prevention in Communities and Tribes.

Background: Improving incorporation of pollution prevention activities, tools and policies into community and tribal advocacy strategies requires a concerted effort to build tribal and community capacity to participate. Communities and tribes must be active partners in pollution prevention planning activities in order to help identify priorities and measure progress. To participate on a level playing field, communities and tribes must have adequate and sustained funding from public and private sources to support their efforts. Educational materials suitable for the layman must be developed and comprehensive educational training initiatives should be undertaken. For example, EPA supported pollution prevention capacity-building for the Common Sense Initiative, Printing Sector, New York City Community Education Project that empowered community groups to approach local printers with pollution prevention materials for printers and information on process and product changes. The US EPA has a policy that recognizes a government-to-government responsibility in the implementation of EPA programs on reservations. Tribes, tribal colleges and Native organizations also must have adequate and sustained funding from public and private sources to support these efforts.

Actions items:

a. Provide resources to facilitate community and tribal participation in pollution prevention projects.

b. Utilize and widely disseminate pertinent educational materials already developed and translated into other languages.

c. Develop a Citizen Primer for Pollution Prevention technologies and strategies accessible to the laymen. Utilize pertinent materials already developed.

d. Create a pollution prevention-training academy for communities including a mobile academy that uses a cooperative approach among academic institutions, public and private training institutions, and resource centers, especially those designed for the environmental justice communities. This training should be inclusive of national and international laws that provide guidance in protection of rights and resources.

e. Create a pollution prevention-training academy for tribes, tribal colleges and Native organizations.

f. Compile a collection of case studies with viable examples featuring community and tribal representation in pollution prevention. Collaborations would be useful as an example of successful pollution prevention partnerships. A clearinghouse with the case studies could be placed on a Website. The multi-stakeholder collaborative model, once developed, should be provided to local governments and community organizations. The model will detail the steps to an effective community involvement process in pollution prevention projects.

g. Where appropriate, compliance penalties in environmental justice communities should be directed to pollution prevention projects that benefit the health, environment and quality of life of community members, rather than directing these funds to state and local general funds, or to the U.S. Treasury. Community members and facility employees should oversee these projects jointly in order to assure that community needs are met and improved collaboration between the penalized facility and its neighbors is facilitated.

I-3. Strengthen Implementation of Pollution Prevention Programs on Tribal Lands and Alaskan Native Villages.

Background: Tribal governments, tribal communities and Alaska Native villages face significant challenges in safeguarding their lands and treaty protected tribal resources on and off the reservations. When a viable tool to assist tribal governments in fulfilling their duty is available, it should be shared among the tribes and considered for adoption. The National Tribal Environmental Council (NTEC), an inter-tribal organization comprised of some 170 tribes, provides an important mechanism for sharing information on successful tribal government programs, through its annual conferences, its web site and other means.

Many other organizations can serve as resources for educational programs and for sharing information, including the Institute for Tribal Environmental Professionals (ITEP) at Northern Arizona University and the National Tribal Environmental Research Institute (NTERI), operated by the Inter Tribal Council of Arizona. NTEC, ITEP, and NTERI are some of the key entities supported by EPA to provide assistance to tribes.

Tribes generally support the concept of pollution prevention as it already has a long history in tribal cultural practices. Pollution prevention is key to preserving tribal resources on and off the reservations and is consistent with tribal values that encourage planning for future generations.

Tribal governments and Alaska Natives are increasing economic opportunities through partnerships with business and industry, often with federal program support. Many tribes and Alaska Natives are using their natural resources to sustain the tribes economically. Tribal reservations and Alaska Native lands contain a wealth of resources and minerals from agriculture, timber, water, oil and gas reserves, low-sulfur coal and uranium. Pollution prevention activities with industry on tribal and Alaska Native lands must address these industrial activities and their associated environmental impacts. Pollution prevention is also applicable to efforts to prevent pollution from commercial agriculture, resource extraction, transportation and other industrial developments in tribal lands. This should include establishing partnerships to develop research projects, providing technical direction and administrative support for selected pollution prevention projects and developing new methods and technologies that would save energy, reduce waste and emissions.

One example is the Alaskan Native Resources Group that also uses pollution prevention as a tool to preserve and protect their Alaska Native villages and environment. The Alaskan Native Resources has used pollution prevention education to protect future generations from environmental hazards. The Group cites that pollution prevention is a simple method of following the Three R's. The three R's are:

- Reducing purchases that will become wastes (this is consumer source reduction or waste prevention)
- Reusing purchases before discarding them as trash
- Recycling[46]

The Indigenous Environmental Network, a national Native environmental justice organization, taking a lead from the mid 1990's Earth Ambassadors initiative of the United National Indian Tribal Youth program have incorporated a fourth "R", that being Respect. This is based upon most tribal philosophy of a connection to good things coming in four and for all people to have more respect for the earth and environment.

---

[46] "Pollution Prevention." Alaskan Native Resources. 29 July 2002. http://www.alaskanativeresources.com/p2.html.

Action items:

a. EPA should provide or offer assistance to tribal governments who need to fill the enforcement gap by Direct Implementation of Tribal Cooperative Agreements ("DITCAs").

b. EPA should offer assistance to tribal governments in the drafting and implementing of Tribal Environmental Policy Acts ("TEPAs") that include pollution prevention requirements.

c. EPA should provide or offer assistance to tribal governments to engage in land use planning and economic development activities under tribal law that promote pollution prevention activities on tribal lands.

d. EPA should provide or offer assistance to tribal governments to develop strategies for incorporating pollution prevention in development projects including walkable neighborhoods, smart growth principles, and geographic information system technologies to assist in land use analysis and planning.

e. EPA should provide or offer assistance to tribes, tribal education institutions and Native organizations to institute educational programs to advance pollution prevention in and near tribal lands.

f. EPA should work with other federal agencies to provide or offer assistance to tribes to promote pollution prevention initiatives in industrial development such as mineral extraction activities operating within and near the lands of tribes and Alaska Native villages.

g. EPA should provide or offer assistance to tribal governments to develop memorandum of understandings ("MOU") with adjoining governmental entities such as states or municipalities. These MOUs can also be generally helpful in addressing pollution prevention issues and implementing pollution prevention programs. EPA should investigate the extent to which such agreements already exist and whether such existing agreements can be used as a model.

I-4. Promote Efforts to Institutionalize Pollution Prevention Internationally, Particularly in Developing Countries.

Background: Pollution does not recognize political or jurisdictional boundaries. As a result pollution generated locally has national and international impacts. There is a need for increased global environmental protection as well as enhanced economic development in developing countries. These needs (for protecting the environment and continued economic development) must be balanced and the tradeoffs between the two objectives minimized. This requires that governments, industries, and citizens —at home and abroad— stop viewing pollution and resource depletion as inevitable by-products of "progress." Additionally, the stakeholders should work to incorporate environmental management into all levels of decision-making. This requires a focus on preventing pollution *before it occurs*, and making the most efficient use of existing natural resources. Measures to address pollution prevention should be promoted on an international level with a special focus on developing countries in order to assist these countries to improve their standards of living in more sustainable ways than many of those chosen by the developed nations.

In efforts to involve all levels of decision-makers in measures to promote pollution prevention, special attention should be directed to the circumstances of indigenous peoples. In many parts of the world, polluting industries such as mineral extraction take place within the aboriginal territories of indigenous peoples, often without any legal requirement for informed consent of such peoples. An emerging body of international law, including human rights law, recognizes the rights of indigenous peoples to maintain their own ways of life within their aboriginal homelands, which necessarily includes a substantial degree of autonomous self-government in matters such as environmental and natural resource management.[47] In many countries, however, national law provides little or no protection for the rights of indigenous peoples. Pollution prevention offers a range of ways to avoid imposing environmental damage on indigenous peoples, and special efforts should be pursued to engage them in pollution prevention initiatives.

The USAID's Global Development Alliance has been developed to combine international assets of governments, business and civil society to work in partnership in implementing sustainable development programs in developing nations. The GDA seeks to serve as a catalyst to mobilize the ideas, efforts, and resources of the public sector, corporate America and non-governmental organizations[1] in support of shared objectives. The International Joint Commission (created by the US and Canada) oversees water quality in the rivers and lakes that lie along or flow across the United States-Canada Border. The two countries cooperate to manage and protect these waters. The Commission established the International Air Quality Advisory Board to identify and provide advice on air pollution issues with transboundary implications. The North American Agreement on Environmental Cooperation (NAAEC) to address regional environmental concerns, to prevent potential conflicts between trade and environmental protection interests, and to promote the effective enforcement of environmental law, established the Commission for Environmental Cooperation (CEC).

Efforts also are needed to improve the environmental quality and affordability of products distributed throughout the world. Major U.S. corporations including Dow, Dupont, Hewlett Packard, Coca Cola, Johnson and Johnson, Pfizer, and Timberland, as well as non-U.S. companies such as Unilever are currently engaged in initiatives to market environmentally sound products in developing countries. EPA can play a role in encouraging and providing information on initiatives to provide the world with needed,

---

[47] See generally S. James Anaya, Indigenous Peoples in International Law (1996).

high quality, environmentally benign products at affordable cost. These activities not only reduce world pollution, but they seek to extend economic vitality to all.

Actions items:

a. Promote sustainable consumption and production patterns both locally and on an international level.

b. Continue the establishment and support cleaner production programs and centers. Additionally, the concept of waste minimization circles and clubs (currently in India, South Africa and Europe) can be expanded to involve greater community participation. This strategy could help to improve the profitability of SMEs and be an integral part of local poverty reduction strategies.

c. Continue cooperation with the CEC for implementation of pollution prevention programs in North American countries.

d. Expand U.S. technical assistance program to governments for development of environmental protection policies, regulations and laws.

e. Review existing federal program to identify ways to assist indigenous peoples in realizing the potential benefits of pollution prevention, through technical assistance for sustainable development within indigenous communities and through measures to avoid imposing environmental burdens on indigenous peoples in order to provide benefits for others.

II. MORE EFFECTIVE UTILIZATION OF TOOLS AND PROGRAMS

II-1. Identify and Implement Opportunities to Advance Environmental Justice through Pollution Prevention in Federal Environmental Statutes.

Background:

The Pollution Prevention Act of 1990 (42 U.S.C.A. §§13101-13109) was enacted to shift the practices for controlling air emissions, water effluents, and the treatment of waste, from end-of-pipe approaches to the reduction of pollution at the source. The hierarchy of preferred approaches included changes in inputs/starting materials, final product reformulation, and process redesign. The Act was passed in the same year as the Clean Air Amendments that heralded more stringent control of air pollution.

The Pollution Prevention Act was not just one more piece of legislation in the armament available to EPA. Section 13103(a) of the Act required EPA to establish a "[pollution prevention] office independent of the Agency's single-media program offices" and §13103(b)(2) required EPA to develop and implement a strategy to promote source reduction. Specifically, the Administrator was required to:

> ensure that the Agency considers the effect of its existing and proposed programs on source reduction efforts and shall review regulations of the Agency prior and subsequent to their proposal to determine their effects on source reduction…

The mandated oversight and coordinating role for EPA under the authority of the Pollution Prevention Act was never fully implemented. The Environmental Law Institute (ELI), in 1993, issued a report on opportunities to advance pollution prevention in federal environmental statutes. That report identified opportunities in the Clean Water Act and the Resource Conservation and Recovery Act for incorporating pollution prevention tools into management of environment resources. In 2001, ELI developed another report on opportunities to advance environmental justice under federal environmental statutes. EPA could benefit from a more critical look at specific opportunities to advance pollution prevention to address environmental justice issues, particularly in, but not limited to the permitting process.

Environmental quality review statutes also offer opportunities to incorporate pollution prevention at the beginning stages of development projects. Use of Tribal Environmental Policy Acts (TEPA's) may be a useful tool to explore this avenue. For example, the Oneida Tribe of Wisconsin is developing a TEPA with an EPA Environmental Justice Pollution Prevention Grant. However there is no reason that new actions governed by national and state environmental policy acts cannot also require pollution prevention measures in new buildings and development projects as a condition for approval

37

consistent with the underlying goals of these acts to assure the environmental managers and regulators behave as stewards for future generations.

There are also opportunities for states to improve compliance using pollution prevention. The Environmental Protection Agency published a document in 1998 detailing ways to incorporate pollution prevention measures in permitting, enforcement and inspection in delegated programs. This document, *Pollution Prevention Solutions During Permitting, Inspections and Enforcement*, includes seventy-one concrete examples of how states have used pollution prevention to help companies meet or exceed compliance requirements in all media areas and across all media.

Actions items:

a. EPA should review existing federal environmental statutes to identify avenues to increase pollution prevention and should identify and explore impediments to integrating pollution prevention using existing regulatory directives. EPA's review should list avenues or mechanisms identified, impediments found and approaches to overcome barriers identified.

b. EPA should staff and empower the Office of Pollution Prevention to carry out its original mandate to review past and future regulations for their effects on source reduction.

c. EPA should encourage the states to review existing source reduction opportunities in the context of state permit issuance, enforcement and inspection programs for increased opportunities for source reduction and identify impediments for incorporating source reduction at the state level. Review by the states should detail opportunities identified and employed to implement source reduction measures and describe steps examined and undertaken to overcome impediments to increasing source reduction at the state level. EPA should provide some idea of a regulatory framework to accomplish this task.

d. EPA should, in consultation with tribes, review the implementation of federal environmental statutes within Indian country to identify ways to integrate pollution prevention into aspects of federal statutes that EPA implements directly and to encourage tribes to integrate pollution prevention into those programs for which they have primary authority. EPA should also provide assistance to tribes that choose to promote pollution prevention through tribal laws, such as Tribal Environmental Policy Acts.

e. EPA should instigate a review of federal and state pollution prevention measures for duplication and eliminate duplication where possible.

II-2. Promote Local Area Multi-Media, Multi-Hazard Reduction Planning and Implementation.

Background: Multiple sources of pollutants raise concerns because they may be concentrated in densely populated geographic areas where large numbers of people may be exposed. EPA recognizes that pollutants come from new and existing sources and in many cases from the cumulative contribution of sources including hazardous emissions from large and small businesses, agricultural run-off and other non-point water pollution sources and transportation related sources. Pollution prevention should target local sources with effective solutions. In order to accomplish this goal, toxics reduction plans should be developed that reduce overall pollution levels equitably in geographic areas covered by the plans, and assure that potential increases are not disproportionately borne, local areas covered by the plans should receive benefits and incentives, and the public should be meaningfully included in the development, implementation and evaluation of the plans. In addition, hazard reduction in industrial facilities, a key concern for environmental justice communities, EPA and the nation as a whole, should be addressed.

The potential of these efforts is enormous. More than 113 million lbs/yr (56,500 tons/yr) of hazardous chemicals and more than 152 million lbs (76,000 tons to date) of solvents have been eliminated through Green Chemistry initiatives. This includes elimination of CFC and VOC solvents as well as persistent, toxic, and bioaccumulating chemicals. These programs have also saved 55 million gallons/yr of water, saved 88.9 trillion BTU/yr of energy, and eliminated 57 million lbs/yr of carbon dioxide emissions.[48]

Action Items:

a. Local areas with multiple sources of pollution should develop toxics reduction plans that reduce overall levels of pollution and allow for assimilative capacity while assuring that overall toxic levels are going down. These plans should distinguish between permitted and non-permitted sources and activities and include proposals for source reduction and elimination. A key component of these plans should be creation of an inventory of specific sources of toxic exposure covered by the plan including the amounts of pollution released into the environment. This inventory should be developed with information from EPA as well as from environmental and health departments of state, tribal and local governments.

b. Toxics reductions plans should encourage state, local and tribal governments to use the broadest possible set of strategies to reduce air emissions, water pollutants and/or solid and hazardous waste that impact upon communities at risk. Actions can be source specific or community based and local planning and land use issues should be incorporated into these plans. Plans can be based upon voluntary actions or existing statutory authority to require specific reductions from new or

---

[48] Mary Kirchhoff, The Green Chemistry Institute.

existing sources, to assure that new sources in the area still result in overall reductions in pollution and to assure the consideration of health impacts of exposure reductions and increases. Plans should identify opportunities to include pollution prevention in permitted facilities. Plans should include measures to prevent or eliminate potential unacceptable impacts. Plans should use the myriad of EPA and other methods and approaches in multi-hazard reduction planning.

c.   Toxics reduction plans should include measurable goals and mechanisms for addressing overburdened areas and reducing pollution from permitted and non-permitted sources. Goals developed should be explicit, measurable, equitable and consistent with existing statutory and regulatory requirements. Goals should be developed in coordination with residents of the affected communities, and once developed, activities should be selected and measures should be chosen to achieve the goals of the plan while including the impacted community as a key partner.

d.   Toxics reduction plans should include the affected community and keep the community informed of progress in achieving the goals of the plans. This can be done by providing regular progress reports and creating a public forum where the reports can be discussed. The community covered by the plan must be given sufficient information in advance to meaningfully review and comment on the plans. Communities should also be involved in updating and evaluating the success of the plans. Options for measuring the success of the plans can include ambient and/or source monitoring, inventory tracking and activity tracking.

e.   State, tribal and local governments that develop and implement multi-hazard toxics reduction plans using a multistakeholder collaborative model should be eligible to receive administrative benefits as incentives for development of the plans. These benefits can include regulatory flexibility, financial support and recognition.

II-3. Promote efforts to incorporate Pollution Prevention and Environmental Justice in Supplemental Environmental Projects (SEPs).

Background: A SEP is an environmentally beneficial project, not otherwise required by law, which an individual, corporation or government entity (entity) agrees to perform in settlement of an enforcement action. In exchange for the legal commitment to undertake a SEP, a percentage of the cost of the SEP may be considered as a factor in establishing the penalty paid. Both the United States Environmental Protection Agency (EPA) and many states promote the use of SEPs. SEPs may arise in the contexts of either: (1) an EPA initiated enforcement action or (2) the voluntary self-disclosure of a violation under the EPA Audit Policy. In the EPA led enforcement context, SEPs conform to the EPA SEP Policy of May 1, 1998. SEPs must meet certain requirements for EPA to enter into a settlement agreement that includes a SEP. By far the most limiting of these requirements is the need for "nexus" between the violation and the proposed project. A nexus exists if: (1) the project is designed to reduce the likelihood that similar violations will reoccur; (2)

40

the project reduces adverse impacts to public health or the environment from the violation; or (3) the project reduces overall risk to public health or the environment from the violation.

Pollution Prevention SEPs involve changes that reduce or eliminate some form of pollution, or reduce pollutants, toxicity prior to recycling, treatment, or disposal. In the context of SEPs, pollution prevention is synonymous with source reduction. Examples of pollution prevention SEPs have included: use of less toxic materials to make products; modifications in the production process to reduce materials losses; changes in product design which require less pollution processes; and improved housekeeping. Pollution Prevention SEPs that implement source reductions are especially favored.

Pollution prevention assessments, which fall within the broader category of "Assessments and Audits," are systematic, internal reviews of specific processes and operations designed to identify and provide information about opportunities to reduce the use, production, and generation of toxic and hazardous materials and other wastes. To be eligible for SEPs, such assessments must be conducted using a recognized pollution prevention assessment or waste minimization procedure to reduce the likelihood of future violations. Pollution prevention assessments are acceptable as SEPs without a specific commitment to implementation. Implementation is not required because drafting implementation requirements before the results of an assessment are known is difficult.

The EPA SEP Policy emphasizes the value of "SEPs in communities where environmental justice concerns are present...". However, "[b]ecause environmental justice is not a specific technique or process but an overarching goal, it is not listed as a particular SEP category; but EPA encourages SEPs in communities where environmental justice may be an issue." In addition, the EPA SEP Policy explicitly encourages community participation in the SEP development process, by recognizing that, "[s]oliciting community input into the SEP development process can: result in SEPs that better address the needs of the impacted community; promote environmental justice; produce better community understanding of EPA enforcement; and improve relations between the community and the violating facility.

Actions items:

a. Improve coordination and efficiency of activities through increased programmatic integration of Audit Policy, compliance assistance, pollution prevention SEPs, and environmental justice activities.

b. Improve quality of SEPs, increase community participation and reduce transaction cost to SEP agreement by implementation of SEP-Pollution Prevention training designed for different stakeholder groups, implementation of SEP-Pollution Prevention Library; and finalizing the draft "EPA Guidance for Community Involvement in Supplemental Environmental Projects," 65 Fed. Reg. 40639-40644 (June 30, 2000).

c. Increase the number of Pollution Prevention-Environmental Justice SEPs by encouraging states, tribes, and municipalities to establish SEP policies; establishing system of incentives both within EPA and outside; and increasing communication between EPA Regional SEP coordinators and EPA Regional Environmental Justice Coordinators.

d. Create market based Pollution Prevention SEP through which the entity could purchase/fund pollution prevention initiatives at non-entity or off-site facilities benefiting the impacted low-income and or minority communities or other community with an appropriate nexus.

e. Quantify results of Pollution Prevention-Environmental Justice SEPs through tracking and monitoring to identify the type and level of use of Pollution Prevention-Environmental Justice SEPs and enhance compliance with SEP terms and determine actual levels or pollution reductions.

II-4. Provide Incentives to Promote Collaboration Among Communities, Business and Government on Pollution Prevention Projects in Environmental Justice Communities.

Background: Communities, business and government should form partnerships to implement and sustain pollution prevention programs that target environmental justice communities. EPA can facilitate these cooperative efforts directly and by encouraging states to engage in pollution prevention programs and outreach efforts. Government can provide incentives for communities to embrace pollution prevention solutions by providing resources for capacity building, disseminating written information concerning pollution prevention, and considering input from and environmental risks to communities when issuing permits and setting standards in targeted communities. Government incentives to businesses to engage in collaborative pollution prevention efforts may include drafting flexible conditions or pollution prevention compliance options in permits, employing innovative pilot programs, and providing technical assistance. Government can also encourage businesses implementing private programs such as the chemical industry's Responsible Care to focus on pollution prevention initiatives for environmental justice communities.

An example of a flexible permitting process that creates mutual benefit to communities and manufacturers is a Project XL program undertaken by Merck & Co. Merck reduced air emission levels in Elkton, Virginia by converting its coal-burning powerhouse to natural gas. Use of a cleaner burning fuel enhanced visibility and reduced acid deposition in the local community and a national park. In exchange, Merck received a site-wide emissions cap that allowed it to make changes at the facility without obtaining further regulatory approval as long as the cap was not exceeded.

Action Items:

a. EPA, in partnership with states and tribes, should implement pollution prevention program and outreach efforts that target environmental justice communities. EPA should provide incentives to communities to participate in collaborative pollution prevention activities by offering resources for capacity building, disseminating literature and written information concerning pollution prevention and considering input from and environmental risks to communities when issuing permits and setting standards. Literature should include plain English and multi-lingual descriptions of pollution prevention resources. Permitting processes should include discussions among communities, business and government of opportunities to implement pollution prevention. EPA should designate within its Office of Enforcement and Compliance Assistance a knowledgeable technical assistance staff to coordinate EPA outreach efforts and facilitate dialogue among the community, business and government, help identify specific pollution prevention projects suitable for the community, and educate companies and communities about the existence of proven, cost-effective technologies and innovation opportunities.

b. EPA should identify "priority pollution prevention communities" based upon the risk posed to communities from the aggregation of polluting sources. This initiative should focus on communities of color and low-income communities, thereby reflecting the stated commitment of EPA to environmental justice. EPA should provide compliance assistance and pollution reduction and elimination incentives targeted at activities within these communities.

c. EPA should develop and implement programs, initiatives and incentives to encourage businesses to engage in collaborative partnerships to implement pollution prevention, use green technologies and non-toxic materials and design innovative processes in minority and low-income communities. These incentives may include special recognition of the business for its pollution prevention activities; low interest loans or grants for research into pollution prevention solutions to community risks; expedited permitting; consolidated multi-media reporting; flexible, multi-media, facility-wide permits with a single agent point of contact; "smart permits" that authorize a range of operating scenarios contemplated by the company obtaining the permit; compliance options in permits based on pollution prevention technologies or innovation; and increased emissions reduction credits or higher trading ratios where pollution prevention is used in the context of an emissions trading program to reduce pollution in an environmental justice community. EPA should also communicate pollution prevention ideas to industry sectors through trade associations, an integrated website, or other means and enhance the existing pollution prevention Roundtable. EPA should encourage groups supporting corporate environmental reporting (GEMI, the Conference Board, UNEP, ISO) to include separate line item reporting on pollution prevention in environmental justice communities.

d. EPA should initiate, and encourage states and tribes to initiate, programs to assist small businesses in developing and implementing pollution prevention activities including source reduction, waste minimization and recycling.

e. EPA should facilitate the formation of government-private sector partnerships to encourage businesses that cannot eliminate wastes to recycle them. EPA should develop programs to increase the volume of recyclable and reusable materials collected from public and private sources (e.g. electronics and paper from businesses and consumers). EPA should provide incentives to increase use of products made from recyclable materials. Without product use, collection of recyclables is unsustainable.

III. SUSTAINABLE PROCESSES AND PRODUCTS

III-1. Encourage "Green Buildings," "Green Businesses," and "Green Industries" through EPA's Brownfields and Smart Growth programs.

Background: Businesses, communities, and tribes share a common interest in returning properties with actual or potential environmental contamination to productive use. Brownfield projects, which by their nature often reduce pollution by remediating and reusing formerly impacted properties, routinely incorporate dialogue with neighboring community members to identify their goals for site response and reuse, whether these projects are coordinated by EPA, states or performed independently under the ASTM standard for brownfields. The new brownfields legislation, the Small Business Liability Relief and Brownfields Revitalization Act, encourages environmentally friendly redevelopment through brownfields grant selection criteria, e.g. "The Administrator shall establish a system for ranking grant applications received under this paragraph that includes... [t]he extent to which a grant would facilitate the use or reuse of existing infrastructures." EPA has also been active in facilitating recreational community enrichment projects, such as converting brownfields into community parks and recreation fields, where is has been demonstrated that contamination no longer exists. EPA currently is developing guidance for implementation of the Brownfields Revitalization Act to clarify that cleanups undertaken under these programs will incorporate robust public participation measures, such as those included in the ASTM Standard Guide for Process of Sustainable Brownfields Redevelopment. (November 1, 1998).[49]

Projects should address equity issues and promote green industries development as well as the use of existing infrastructure. One such "green building" brownfields development is a project by Bethel New Life project in Chicago. Similarly, EPA worked with community group members, local government, the school district and the site owner to transform the closed, remediated H.O.D. landfill and its buffer property into a multi-use recreational facility. Efforts were made to ensure that no further contamination from the

---

[49] ASTM Standard Guide for Process of Sustainable Brownfields Redevelopment., November1, 1998.

landfill would impact the new walking and running trails, ball fields and a planned ecological education laboratory. To assure long-term environmental protection and provide "green energy," landfill gas collected at the closed facility will be collected and used to heat school buildings and homes. In additional examples, New York state remediation projects, which benefit the environment and have potential for public or recreational use of cleaned up property, are eligible for grants.

Actions items:

a. EPA, in cooperation with other federal agencies, should provide clear, readily accessible information to encourage new development, construction or redevelopment. These efforts should include green building materials, sustainable energy options and sustainable transportation options.

b. Brownfields projects should use the opportunity to reuse land to support more sustainable use of the land that does not leave contamination for future generations. One way to do this would be to encourage and promote a green business development component in projects receiving the support of government.

c. EPA should give full weight to criteria that encourages environmentally friendly development in the new Brownfields Law.

d. EPA's assistance to tribes on brownfields cleanup and redevelopment should encourage "green buildings," "green businesses," and "green industries."

III-2. Promote Product Substitution and Process Substitution in Areas which Impact Low-income, Minority and Tribal Communities.

Background: Society depends upon chemicals to provide it with a wide range of consumer products, from life-saving pharmaceuticals to plastic food containers, which make up the fabric of our everyday lives. Yet the manufacture of chemicals has created some unintended environmental consequences. The use of chlorofluorocarbons (CFCs) in air conditioners, refrigerators, and aerosol cans has catalyzed the destruction of stratospheric ozone. Combustion of fossil fuels has been linked to global climate change. Industrial releases of pollutants have damaged both human health and the environment.

There have been a variety of initiatives to promote product and process substitution in low-income communities and communities of color. In order to maintain standard of living while protecting human health and the environment, fundamental changes are required in the area of product and process substitution, focusing on the design of chemical products and processes that reduce or eliminate the use and generation of hazardous substances. Human health and environmental benefits can be realized by designing toxicity and hazard out of the chemical manufacturing process. This is a classic example of how pollution prevention can be used in environmental justice communities to bring about positive change.

The "Healthy Home and Healthy School" projects, through product substitution of lead based paints with non-toxic paints have made strides in reducing lead levels in the homes and schools of environmental justice communities. The Janitorial Products Pollution Prevention Project found that use of hazardous products could be reduced by 13% per year if janitors used fewer chemicals, substituted less toxic chemicals, installed mats, vacuumed and avoided aerosol products. Another area of concern is in pest control. Dow AgroSciences developed a targeted approach to termite control using a highly selective insect growth regulator that disrupts the molting process in termites. [50] This breakthrough replaces typical termite treatments that use large quantities of insecticide to form a barrier around a structure. By switching to a targeted bait system, worker exposure to large volumes of insecticide is reduced and potential contamination of wells and ponds is avoided. Similarly, Cleary Chemical Corporation designed a Nutritional Metabolism Disruptor to block the formation of uric acid, a vital component in cockroach metabolism and reproduction. This technology eliminates the need for conventional chemical insecticides, providing a safer option for controlling cockroaches, which pose a significant health problem in low-income communities.

Actions items:

a. Develop "Cleaning for Health" or "Healthy Home and Healthy School" projects, including schools within Indian reservations.

b. Replicate and expand innovative pollution prevention technical assistance projects (such as the current dry cleaner, auto body repair, printer pollution prevention, and integrated pest management projects).

c. Target facilities and activities for which pollution prevention through product substitution is needed.

d. Document the success of these projects and widely disseminate material on product alternatives, reductions and substitutions.

e. Analyze obstacles to the replication of innovative pollution prevention technical assistance in tribal communities and devise strategies to overcome such obstacles.

III-3. Promote Just and Sustainable Transportation Projects and Initiatives.

Background: Just and sustainable transportation strategies focus on ways to assure that all people have access to high quality and affordable transportation systems. These will maximize the use of the cleanest, least polluting, and least resource-intensive vehicle technologies and fuels. These will provide expanding choices for people and businesses

---

[50] Mary Kirchhoff, The Green Chemistry Institute

to move themselves and freight in an environmentally sound way. Similarly, they would enable communities and economies in a planned manner so as to function with less need to move people and goods. These strategies are critical for improving the quality of life of minority, low income and tribal communities and other transportation disadvantaged and sensitive populations such as those with respiratory illnesses, the elderly, the disabled, and children, which historically receive the least benefits of adequate transportation systems while often bearing the greatest burdens.

While only 8% percent of American households do not own motor vehicles on average, that number jumps to approximately 22% for black families. Also approximately 80% of all vehicle-less households earn less than $25,000 annually. This makes access to clean, affordable mass transportation an area of concern from an environmental justice perspective. Programs that promote building of transit oriented communities (land use), reducing the cost of mass transit use (commuter choice) and retrofitting of the existing transit fleet with cleaner engines (retrofit) help assure that all people have access to high quality and affordable transportation systems.

Important pollution prevention challenges in the area of transportation from an environmental justice perspective include meaningful community involvement in the transportation planning process and proper consideration of land use issues. Additionally, greater utilization of environmental friendly and non-polluting vehicle technologies and tools would help address potentially adverse and disproportionate air quality and other environmental and health impacts from transportation related pollution.

Due to Clean Air Act requirements for cleaner vehicles, engines, and fuels today the average new car is forty percent cleaner than in 1990. Everyday, across nation, clean air programs prevent 600 premature deaths; 2,000 cases of chronic illness such as asthma and bronchitis; 300,00 cases of minor respiratory illness such as aggravated asthma; and 75,000 people from missing work. However air pollutants still present a significant health risk. The Journal of the American Medical Association recently found that airborne pollutants generated by diesel-powered vehicles caused reduced lung function, lung damage, increased asthma attacks and premature mortality. According to a report by The Center for Disease Control and Prevention in Atlanta, acute asthma attacks have increased 100% among children in the last fifteen years from 2.3 to 5.5 million.

Action Items:

a. Work in partnership with the U.S. Department of Transportation to ensure that impacted communities have meaningful and early participation in and are involved throughout the transportation planning process.

b. Promote the best possible transportation projects and related infrastructure development that enhance community viability and accessibility, both environmentally and economically.

c. Ensure that transportation planning and environmental impact studies consider the impacts of transportation policies and projects and promote use of clean transportation technologies as part of pollution prevention and mitigation measures where impacts are or may be adverse and disproportionate.

d. Provide education and training to air quality and transportation agencies and the public on ways to promote and incorporate use of non-polluting vehicle technologies and clean fuels.

e. Promote greater access to mass transit systems and provide for increased investments in transportation systems that provide better accessibility, particularly for urban low-income and minority communities.

f. Develop public-private partnerships to increase use of non-polluting vehicle technologies and clean fuels.

g. Identify incentives, both monetary and non-monetary, to promote acquisition and use of clean transportation technologies.

h. Increase purchase and use of clean technology and alternative fuel vehicles in government owned vehicular fleets.

i. Work in partnership with BIA and tribal governments to address these issues for tribal communities.

III-4. Improve Opportunities for Pollution Prevention at Federal Facilities

Background: Federal facilities are under an obligation to comply with federal laws, regulations and Presidential Orders that relate to pollution prevention. "Greening" executive orders, including green purchasing, offer the potential to move beyond compliance by reduction of materials use and impacts on natural resources. RCRA § 6002 and Executive Order 13101 require federal facilities to establish programs to purchase environmentally preferable and biobased materials. Federal Acquisition Regulations were amended in the year 2000 to require agencies to demonstrate compliance within their contracts by requiring procurement and use of recycled products designated by EPA and consideration of environmentally preferable products. Federal facilities are required to improve their energy use by Executive Order 13123. This executive order, Greening the Government through Efficient Energy Management, requires more efficient energy use and Energy Star performance rating for buildings in general facility audits.

Pollution prevention is an environmental justice issue for federal facilities as it is for other sectors that generate, store or treat waste and use natural resources. The Federal Facilities Enforcement Office ("FFEO") oversees pollution prevention measures at federal facilities. Important components of FFEO's work that prevent pollution include interagency agreement negotiation support, compliance monitoring, targeting support and technical assistance and capacity building.

FFEO provides pollution prevention training, policy and guidance, funds pilot projects and advocates the use of Environmental Management System Reviews as a way of identifying areas at federal facilities where environmental quality improvements are possible. FFEO also coordinates environmental justice initiatives related to federal facilities with the Regions.

Federal facilities offer a wide range of opportunities to improve environmental performance that can benefit low-income communities, communities of color and tribes, particularly when those facilities are near or in impacted communities. Public information and input on compliance and performance improvements at 800,000 regulated facilities, including federal facilities, has recently been made available through an on-line database, Enforcement and Compliance History Online ("ECHO"), that provides users with detailed facility reports as well as a demographic profile of the surrounding area. This service allows communities to identify facilities in compliance and ascertain where improvements beyond compliance are possible. Examples of pollution prevention successes are detailed in FFEO's FEDFACTS, published by EPA.

Action items:

a. EPA should expand initiatives to improve compliance at federal facilities on Indian lands. Demonstration pollution prevention partnerships should develop with DOI and other agencies whose activities impact upon Indian lands. Workshops that include all stakeholders should be held to improve capacity building and compliance assistance. These workshops should be targeted towards tribal, Bureau of Indian Affairs ("BIA"), Indian Health Service and other federal facilities located on tribal lands interested in improving their environmental performance. Accessible training materials should be developed for impacted communities that identify agency responsibilities and opportunities to address or improve compliance at these facilities. Tribal led Environmental Management Systems Reviews should be held and lead to the development of Memoranda of Understanding that call for compliance assistance site visits at tribal run BIA and other federal facilities on Indian lands. Measurable goals should be articulated in these memoranda and these facilities should be monitored for improvements.

b. EPA, along with FFEO, should examine toxics use and federal facilities in a uniform way in order to identify opportunities for toxics use reduction and should make toxics use reduction a priority. In one recent project, a Sustainability Program, Washington's Fort Lewis reduced energy usage by 39,000 MBTUs at an annual savings of $425,000 per year and significantly reduced greenhouse gases. Another project, undertaken by the Army Center for Health Promotion and Preventative Medicine, looked at mercury use at federal facilities and identified areas where mercury use reductions were possible. Successful projects that reduce toxics use should be showcased and replicated whenever possible.

c. Recycling of formerly used defense sites ("FUDs") should be accelerated in impacted communities in order to reduce risk to those communities from nonsustainable disposal practices and develop economic opportunities there. Accelerated reuse of FUDS increases the return of formerly used contaminated lands into productive sites for the community-- effectively recycling those sites. One such site, Brooks Air Force Base in San Antonio, Texas, was recently issued the first "Ready for Reuse" certificate for a federal facility nationally. Other communities that can benefit from successful reuse of FUDS should be prioritized based upon the impact upon the community and community characteristics so that reuse can be targeted to the most impacted communities that will receive the greatest benefits.

d. Facility compliance records should be reviewed on line. Facilities in compliance should be targeted for pollution prevention improvements, including use of less toxic materials, more efficient energy use, green purchasing, and recycling of formerly used facilities.

e. Facilities that are not in compliance can benefit from environmental management system reviews to identify areas where improvements are possible. Where such reviews indicate areas for improvements, interagency MOUs should be implemented as these agreements can build trust within communities that the facilities are sincerely committed to compliance and improvements beyond compliance.

f. EPA and FFEO should assist facilities to come into and improve compliance through increased interagency agreement negotiation support, compliance monitoring, targeting support, technical assistance and capacity building. Facilities that come into compliance should be encouraged to take measures that improve pollution prevention by going beyond compliance.

III-5. Identify Opportunities to Promote Cleaner Technologies, Cleaner Energy, and Cleaner Production in Industrial and Commercial Enterprises in Environmental Justice Communities.

Background: Cleaner production is a holistic way of designing and consuming products with minimal impacts on health and ecosystems. Cleaner energy involves a transition from non-renewable fuels that increase pollution to renewable energy sources that generate little pollution. Cleaner technologies, cleaner energy and cleaner production extends the concept of pollution prevention to mean:
- Processes and products that conserve raw materials, water and energy;
- Elimination of toxic raw materials;
- Prioritization of renewable ("green") energy sources,

- Reduction of toxic and hazardous emissions;
- Protection of human health and the environment along the entire life cycle of a product (material extraction to ultimate disposal); and,
- Utilization of concepts such as industrial ecology and eco-efficiency that promote careful attention to material flows, the reuse of waste products, and continuous efforts to improve the efficiency of energy and resource use.

Cleaner production is rooted within the concept of a circular, life-cycle vision of the economy, meaning that a product's impacts are considered from raw material extraction through final production and disposal and ways are identified to reduce the negative impacts throughout the whole process. This concept of cleaner production was adopted into "Agenda 21" of the 1992 United Nations Conference on Environmental and Development and is used internationally to characterize production practices geared towards sustainable forms of development.

Cleaner production and cleaner energy can play an important role for pollution prevention proponents in environmental justice and tribal communities in at least six areas.

> First, promoting cleaner production and cleaner energy at existing industrial facilities offers environmental justice communities positive ways of encouraging business/community partnerships that can jointly seek safer, less energy and resource intensive, and more environmentally friendly businesses that stay in communities and continue to offer local jobs. Confronting polluting facilities with confident expectations that there are alternative technologies and processes that can be adopted within the production operations that would reduce or eliminate the worst hazards offers environmental justice advocates a valuable "solution-oriented" perspective on how to work directly with local businesses

> Second, using cleaner production concepts as decision specifications provides a means of promoting employment opportunities and economic returns on Brownfields development sites without reinvesting in the kind of production facilities that originally created those contaminated sites. Where environmental justice advocates have the opportunity to participate in decision-making about the future uses of Brownfield sites or other abandoned industrial facilities, they should urge that only firms guaranteeing the highest state-of-the-art clean technologies and practices should be considered for those future developments.

> Third, cleaner energy production means relying on decentralized forms of energy generation that derive energy directly from renewable sources (wind, solar or biomass) rather than non-renewable sources (fossil fuels) that must be mined from the earth's crust. Distributed energy generation sources means that lower income neighborhoods can generate energy off the grid and away from centralized fuel-fired power plants. Wind and solar energy generation means reduced levels of pollution from coal and oil fired energy generation facilities that are often sited in

51

environmental justice communities. Reduced reliance on oil, natural gas, coal, and nuclear energy reduces the need to explore, mine and pump in rural areas and on Tribal lands.

Fourth, energy conservation and cleaner fuels can encourage the diffusion of the next generation of transportation systems that prioritizes mass transit and decreases reliance on single passenger motor vehicles that congest highways and increase the pollution that harms the public health and diminishes the environmental quality of inner city and low-income communities.

Fifth, cleaner production offers a means of reducing the hazards of products and services commonly consumed in native and cultural minority communities. These include products and services like pesticides in foods, allergens in paints and adhesives, diesel exposure from trucks and buses, solvents in cleaning chemicals, and toxins in cosmetics and hair care products. Local community leaders should carefully assess the multiple sources of environmental hazards in their neighborhoods and press local businesses, government agencies and service institutions to change their purchasing and consumption practices so as to buy and use only the least hazardous, most environmentally compatible products and services.

Sixth, cleaner production provides an international vehicle for reducing the likelihood that dangerous products and processes, such as waste management and product recycling, are not simply shipped off-shore to low wage communities in industrializing countries. By building positive, "solution-oriented" programs that cross national boundaries and reach people working in or living near facilities that are linked along a product's life cycle, domestic environmental justice programs can assure that only solutions that benefit all people are acceptable.

Action Items:

a. Develop community/business partnerships with local businesses in environmental justice communities to jointly plan and implement cleaner production programs for adopting cleaner technologies, cleaner forms of energy and cleaner products.

b. Establish the principles of cleaner technologies, cleaner energy, and cleaner production as decision criteria for selecting businesses and production processes that would be encouraged as new investments in Brownfield redevelopment programs. Encourage community involvement in the identification of appropriate locations to site clean, renewable energy technologies.

c. Inventory common products sold in environmental justice communities, assess their environmental attributes, and, where possible, work with local retailers to supply less hazardous and more environmentally friendly products.

d. Promote the use of recycled products and secondary materials in local businesses and institutions in order to reduce the need for mining virgin materials or producing new synthetic materials.

e. Encourage the participation of low-income, minority and Tribal communities in the purchase of cleaner energy through blended or block products or green energy certificates that promote market transitions towards renewable energy sources.

f. Promote energy conservation programs such as federal, state and local low-income weatherization programs, the Commuter Choice Leadership Program, the Green Vehicle Guide, and the Clean Air Transportation Communities Grants to reduce the negative health impacts on inner city neighborhoods of oil derived fuel consumption in motor vehicles.

g. Provide assistance to tribal government in using their sovereign powers to promote renewable energy and energy conservation in tribal communities, including support for the development of model tribal laws and educational programs for tribal attorneys.

h. Assure that environmental programs that improve public health and safety in environmental justice communities do not simply transfer hazardous operations to communities elsewhere, particularly to low wage communities in industrializing countries.

i. Promote continued progress in the establishment and implementation of federal efficiency standards for appliances, buildings and vehicles. Encourage financial institutions to work with community interests to develop innovative financial mechanism designed to give low-income communities greater access to clean and efficient energy technologies.

III-6. Optimize and Expand Waste Minimization Activities in Partnership with Communities

Background: The Pollution Prevention Act of 1990 lists, as a matter of national policy, several methods of pollution prevention, including source reduction, recycling, treatment, or environmentally safe disposal or release.[51] When the generation of waste is unavoidable, waste minimization becomes the favored policy. It includes such activities as waste reduction, reuse and recycling (r3). Because pollution may be disproportionately located in environmental justice communities, members of those communities have a strong interest in minimizing waste.

Waste disposal can create many problems for environmental justice communities. More waste means more land acreage is consumed by landfills. More waste means there is a

---

[51] 42 U.S.C. § 13101(b).

greater risk of release of harmful substances to the environment. Household waste often contains some toxic substances that can reach dangerous levels when high volumes of waste are concentrated in landfills. More waste means more trucks may need to enter a community to transport that waste, leading to increased emissions, safety concerns in neighborhoods, and risks of waste spills.

A gap in the in the Resource Conservation and Recovery Act (RCRA) has made municipal waste regulation on tribal reservations an area of special concern. RCRA does not authorize EPA to directly regulate waste but assigns the primary role to the states. Currently, RCRA has not been amended to authorize the treatment of tribes as states.[52] This effectively leaves municipal waste on reservations unregulated.

In the Pollution Prevention Act of 1990, Congress recognized the opportunity for substantial savings to industry in the form of reduced raw materials, pollution control and liability costs, as well as increased environmental protection and decreased worker health and safety risks. Waste minimization can help obtain these savings, especially if incentives are provided to create market demand for waste products or to reduce waste. Many of the options for waste minimization are readily available today and could be encouraged by providing incentives, creating partnerships to share ideas and information, or by educating businesses and communities.

For instance, some states have mandatory municipal recycling programs for aluminum, glass, plastics, paper, and other common materials. Regulatory agencies provide technical assistance, grants, loans and awards to small businesses or communities active in waste minimization. Community composting programs for yard waste are being formed. Companies pay schools and organizations for used printer cartridges and cell phones. The National Waste Minimization Partnership Program encourages the EPA, state and local governments, manufacturers and other commercial companies, and/or non-governmental organizations to form voluntary partnerships that reduce the generation of certain hazardous wastes. These programs are a good start to waste minimization.

Action Items:

    a. EPA should encourage the optimization of current recycling programs and promote the development of comprehensive community recycling plans that may include such programs as composting centers for yard and plant waste, household hazardous waste collection centers, electronic equipment recycling, and the reuse of demolition materials in construction projects.

    b. EPA should encourage technology transfer between governments and industries for recycling technologies or strategies, promote the creation and use of waste

---

[52] Sarah Krakoff, *Tribal Sovereignty and Environmental Justice*, in JUSTICE AND NATURAL RESOURCES: CONCEPTS, STRATEGIES, AND APPLICATIONS, at 161 (Kathryn Mutz, *et al.* eds., Island Press 2002) (discussing the problem of trash disposal in Indian country and the lack of attention to this problem in the environmental justice literature).

minimization plans, and encourage the sharing of this information (allowing for confidential processes to remain confidential).

c. EPA should encourage collaborative partnerships between governments, communities, and businesses to create and implement solutions to waste generation.

d. EPA should encourage businesses to design products that are recyclable or have extended useful lives and promote the reduction of packaging in consumer goods. EPA should encourage businesses to develop product-recycling programs that accept and recycle old products in a safe and responsible manner.

e. EPA should facilitate the creation of incentives for the purchase of recycled materials and work with other agencies within the federal government to offer recycled products as viable alternatives.

f. EPA should identify and eliminate economic barriers to waste minimization, as well as provide incentives and eliminate existing regulatory disincentives to market development for recycled products.

g. EPA should provide technical assistance, grants, and loans to small businesses and communities and educate them in the potential benefits of waste minimization.

h. EPA should provide technical assistance to tribal governments for the regulation of municipal waste.

i. EPA should develop award programs for businesses or communities that achieve excellence or show innovation in waste minimization

j. EPA should investigate impediments in the recycling process that prevent wastes from actually being recycled and develop procedures to overcome these impediments.

PART II: STAKEHOLDER PERSPECTIVES

CHAPTER 3: COMMUNITY PERSPECTIVES

CHAPTER 4: TRIBAL PERSPECTIVES

CHAPTER 5: BUSINESS AND INDUSTRY PERSPECTIVES

CHAPTER 6: GOVERNMENT PERSPECTIVES

CHAPTER 3: COMMUNITY PERSPECTIVES

This chapter was authored by members of the Community Stakeholder group to elaborate on the views of the members of that group, not necessarily reflect the views of members of other stakeholder groups or of the NEJAC Executive Council.

INTRODUCTION

Communities of color, low-income and tribal communities are committed to reducing, eliminating and preventing pollution and its adverse impacts, thereby improving environmental quality where people live, work and play. Impacted communities have viewed pollution prevention (P2) strategies with suspicion because they appear only to manage pollution emissions rather than significantly reducing or eliminating them. Pollution prevention offers tremendous potential to help reduce and eliminate pollution and improve the quality of life in communities. There exists opportunities under existing statutes to advance the goals of pollution prevention and environmental justice. For communities to turn to pollution prevention as a way of addressing environmental inequities, they need to have an established role in the planning and implementation of pollution prevention projects. Recognizing the importance of that role, communities define pollution prevention as it applies to environmental justice as "activities that include community participation and involvement in decision making to reduce, minimize and eliminate pollution through sustainable practices that demonstrate sustainable development and activities." This chapter describes the community perspective on pollution impacts, the potential value of pollution prevention to communities and measures to more fully integrate pollution prevention to advance environmental justice.

Communities understand that existing environmental standards allow some pollution that, at permitted levels, is believed to be safe, but recognize that errors are possible. Scientific uncertainty in many areas is undeniable. In the face of scientific uncertainty measures and policies to reduce pollution should not be narrowly defined and should include use of the precautionary principle. This principle, according to the 1992 Rio Declaration on Environment and Development, states that '[w]hen there are threats of serious or irreversible damage, lack of scientific certainty shall not be used as a reason for postponing cost-effective measures to prevent environmental degradation." The precautionary principle advises that if there are errors, we should err on the side of caution. This means that decisions respecting pollution prevention should be informed by the precautionary principle. Pollution prevention policy-making should include the precautionary principle because both concepts seek to protect the environment, stress proactive and anticipatory action and the assessment of alternatives. Pollution prevention is consistent with the precautionary principle since its aim is to reduce pollution even at levels considered by government to be safe. Innovation in pollution prevention measures

59

or technologies should also employ the precautionary principle for guiding decision-making under conditions of uncertainty.

Pollution prevention lacks the enormous impediments to implementation that are shared by the other approaches requiring legislative action, enforcement or success in litigation. As a concept it has the support of communities. However pollution prevention has many definitions, several definitions vary depending on which stakeholder group is defining pollution prevention, and is used to describe many activities including those that do not involve communities. Pollution prevention could be more accessible to communities if they could see themselves more directly involved and invested in it. For communities to turn to pollution prevention as a way of addressing environmental inequities, they need to have an established role in pollution prevention planning, projects and activities. Recognizing the importance of that role, communities define pollution prevention as it applies to environmental justice as "activities that include community involvement and participation to reduce, minimize and eliminate pollution through sustainable practices that demonstrate sustainable development and activities that go beyond compliance." Communities also need to feel that their role will have an impact on the process rather than being used to play a public relations role. This chapter describes the community perspective on pollution impacts, the value of pollution prevention to communities and measures to more fully integrate pollution prevention to advance environmental justice.

UNDERSTANDING POLLUTION IMPACTS

Communities of color, low-income and tribal communities suffer from numerous adverse pollution impacts from non-sustainable environmental practices that could be reduced or eliminated through pollution prevention measures. These impacts include unfavorable health effects and adverse impacts which are environmental, societal, economic, and international. Reducing all of these adverse impacts from pollution is a key concern of communities that is also shared by the Environmental Protection Agency. The chief goals of the major environmental protection statutes administered by EPA are "protection of public health and the environment". EPA's Framework for Pollution Prevention acknowledges the relationship between preventing adverse health impacts and preventing pollution by stating that partnership with the public health community is a key objective in order to demonstrate that "pollution prevention is disease prevention". [1]

Health and Environmental Impacts

Pollution prevention measures can reduce poor air quality that is believed to contribute to illness and premature death in communities. Outdoor air pollution is responsible for

---

[1] EPA Pollution Prevention Policy Framework, Guiding Social Principles, www.epa.gov/p2/p2ppolicy/framework.htm.

increased morbidity and mortality locally[2] and throughout the world[3]. Research supports the community's view that asthma and other respiratory diseases, cancer, birth defects, liver and kidney damage and premature death, are all attributable, at least in part, to air pollution exposures.[4] Air pollution exposures due to residence in exposure zones of hazardous and other waste sites have also been associated with statistically increased risks of birth defects, breast cancer, and leukemia and bladder cancer.[5]

---

[2] Daniel M. Steigman, Is it "urban" or "asthma?", The Lancet, July 1996, at 143-144 (documenting much higher asthma hospital admission rates in poor and minority communities than in other areas of Boston); R. Charon Gwynn and George D. Thurston, The Burden of Air Pollution: Impacts among Racial Minorities, Environmental Health Perspectives, Volume 109, Supplement 4, August 2001 (exploring disparities in hospital admissions and mortality by race in New York City); Susan M. Bernard, Johnathan M. Samet, Anne Grambsch, Kristie L. Ebi, and Isabelle Romieu, The Potential Impacts of Climate Variability and Change on Air Pollution-Related Health Effects in the United States, Environmental Health Perspectives, Volume 109, Supplement 2, May 2001 (stating that air pollution can cause, respiratory diseases, cardiovascular diseases, alter host defenses, damage lung tissue, lead to premature death and contribute to cancer).

[3] Tom Bellander, Public Health and Air Pollution, The Lancet, January 2001, at 69-70 (estimating the increase of mortality as a result of long term studies of air pollution in Austria, France and Switzerland). Kunzli, N; Kaiser, R; Medina, S; Studnika, M; Chanel, O; Filliger, P; Herry, M; Horak, Jr. F; Puybonnieux-Texier,V; Quenel, P; Schneieder, J; Seethaler, R; Vergnaud, J-C; Sommer, H., Public Health Impact of Outdoor and Traffic Related Air Pollution: A European Assessment, The Lancet, September 2000, at 795-801 (finding that air pollution caused 6% more total mortality, 25,000 new cases of chronic bronchitis in adults, 290,000 additional cases of bronchitis in children, 500,000 more asthma attacks and 16 million person days of restricted activities); Jun Kagawa, Atmospheric Air Pollution Due to Mobile Sources and Effects on Human Health in Japan, Environmental Health Perspectives 102, Supplement 4, October 1994 (finding that unfavorable human health effects result from automobile caused air pollution in large cities and along transportation routes); Tony Sheldon, Reducing Greenhouse Gases Will Have Good Short Tern Effect, British Medical Journal, Volume 321, page 1367, December 2002 (finding that bronchitis in children fell ten percent in relation to reduced concentrations of particulate matter).

[4] Tracey J. Woodruff, Daniel Axelrad, Jane Caldwell, Rachel Morello-Frosch, and Arlene Rosenbaum, Public Health Implications of 1990 Air Toxics Concentrations across the United States, Environmental Health Perspectives, Volume 106, May 1998; Rachel A. Morello-Frosch, Tracey J. Woodruff, Daniel A. Axelrad, Jane C. Caldwell, Air Toxics and Health Risks in California: The Public Health Implications of Outdoor Concentrations, Risk Analysis, Volume 20 Issue 2, February 2000 (predicting 8600 excess cancer cases and for non-cancer health effects a median total hazard index of 17). A national study of air toxics data found that 10% of all census tracts had one or more carcinogenic hazardous air pollutants present in excess of the defined health benchmark concentrations for cancer and non-cancer health effects and over 90% of census tracts had estimated concentrations of benzene, formaldehyde and 1-3 butadiene greater than the cancer health benchmark.

[5] Sandra Geschwind, Jan Stolwijk, Micheal Bracken, Edward Fitzgerald, Alice Stark, Carolyn Olsen, and James Melius, Risk of Congenital Malformations Associated with Proximity to Hazardous Waste Sites, American Journal of Epidemiology, Volume 136, No. 11, 1992 (finding an additional risk of bearing children with birth defects associated with residence near hazardous waste sites); Samuel S. Epstein, Environmental and Occupational Pollutants are Avoidable Causes of Breast Cancer, 24 Int'. J. Health Servs., 145,147, 1994; Elizabeth L. Lewis-Michl, Ph.D., R. Kallenbach, Ph.D., Nannette S. Geary, James M. Melius, M.D., Dr. P.H., Carole L. Ju, M.S.,Maureen F. Orr, M.S., Steven P. Forand, Investigation of Cancer Incidence and Residence Near 38 Landfills with Soil Migration Conditions: New York State 1980-1989 (showing statistically significantly elevated risks for female bladder cancer and female leukemia among women residing in the landfill exposure buffers).

61

Pollution prevention can also reduce the devastating effects of pollution on the environment for plants, animals, marine life and other living things including people who rely on the environment for subsistence food gathering. Some pollutants are persistent (degrade slowly) and bioaccumulate in the environment, often becoming part of the food chain ultimately consumed by people. These types of pollutants, persistent bioaccumulative toxics, are commonly referred to as PBT's. Health effects from subsistence food consumption can translate into extraordinarily high risks for cancer and non-cancer health effects.[6]

Native American and Alaskan Native Nations can benefit from pollution prevention because they are exposed to many of the same environment threats as other communities of color. They suffer from adverse effects of pesticides and other hazardous substances.[7] These exposures result into a variety of adverse health effects including asthma, hypertension, thyroid disorders, cancer and leukemia. Pollution has also impacted upon their ability to engage in traditional cultural practices.[8] However risks to Native Nations are increased because they have not had adequate resources on a government-to-government basis to address those risks.[9]

Societal and Developmental Impacts

Societal and developmental impacts that communities believe that are pollution related can be reduced through pollution prevention. Disparities in socioeconomic status result in health disparities that are exacerbated by environmental exposures.[10] Health care

---

[6] According to the NEJAC Fish Consumption Report, low-income communities, communities of color and tribes have subsistence fish consumption rates ranging from the 90th to the 99th percentile rates for the general population. These fish consumption rates translate into extraordinarily high risks for cancer and non-cancer health effects;Industrial Technology Associates, EPA Cumulative Exposure Assessment for Greenpoint-Williamsburg, 2000 (concluding that total cancer risks from fish consumption range from 1 in 10 to 1 in 1000); Jason Corburn, Combining Community-Based Research and Local Knowledge to Confront Asthma and Subsistence Fishing Hazards in Greenpoint-Williamsburg, Brooklyn, New York, Environmental Health Perspectives Supplements, Volume 110, Number 2, April 2002.

[7] Lorraine Halinka Malcoe, Robert A. Lynch, Michelle Cozier Kegler and Valrie A. Skaggs, Lead Sources, Behaviors and Socioeconomic Factors in Relation to Blood Lead of Native American and White Children, Environmental Health Perspectives Supplements, Volume 110, Number 2, April 2002; Somini Sengupta, A Sick Tribe and a Dump as a Neighbor, The New York Times, April 7, 2001.

[8] U.S. Fish and Wildlife Service, Division of Environmental Quality, Pesticides and Wildlife, Pesticides and Wildlife, July 2001, http://contaminants.fws.gov/Issues/Pesticides.cfm.; Lisa Mastny, Coming to Terms with the Artic, Worldwatch Institute, Worldwatch, Volume 13, p. 24, January 2000.

[9] Mary Arquette, Maxine Cole, Katsi Cook, Brenda LaFrance, Margaret Peters, James Ransom, Elvera Sargent, Vivian Smoke and Arlene Stairs, Holistic Risk-Based Environmental Decision Making: A Native Perspective, Environmental Health Perspectives Supplements, Volume 110, Number 2, April 2002

[10] Nancy E. Alder, and Katherine Newman, Socioeconomic Disparities in Health: Pathways and Policies: Inequality in Education, Income and Occupation Exacerbates the Gaps Between the "Haves" and the "Have-nots", Health Affairs, April 2002

opportunities, health status, educational opportunities, intergenerational transfers of wealth, poverty and lack of health insurance are all measures of socioeconomic status that increase the risk of health disparities and are effected by both race and pollution exposures.[11]

The reduction or elimination of pollution, especially PBTs, would be an effective way to address developmental damage and delay that is more likely to occur when children are exposed to multiple and cumulative risks in their environment.[12] Certain pollutants also have adverse impacts on the reproductive system, and a special concern is endocrine disruptors since they are extremely persistent, bioaccumulate, and therefore have a multi-generational affect. Numerous pollutants targeted for toxic pollution reduction activities, including lead; mercury and polychlorinated biphenyls are neurodevelopment toxicants and cause learning disabilities, attention deficit hyperactivity disorder, developmental delays and emotional and behavioral problems.[13]

Economic Impacts

Communities believe that pollution prevention would be a proactive way to address the adverse economic impacts of pollution that exacerbate poverty and reduce earning ability. Pollution exposure has adverse economic impact on the cost of access to health care in environmental justice communities. Pollution exposures place a huge economic burden on society and just four diseases associated with environmental causation cost the United States and Canada as much as 397 billion dollars a year.[14] There is emerging evidence that there are economic impacts associated with reduced intelligence from pollution exposures. Pollution also jeopardizes property values in impacted communities. Decreased property values translate into loss of equity for use in getting bank loans, and makes it more difficult to sell the property and relocate. Economic data indicates that residence near the fence line of industrial facilities has an adverse economic effect on property values whether or not the property is actually contaminated.[15] Property that is actually contaminated by a nearby source or with contaminated drinking water may be essentially worthless.

---

[11] Id.

[12] Francine Clark Jones, Community Violence, Children and Youth: Considerations For Program, Policy and Nursing Roles, Pediatric Nursing, Volume 23, p. 131, March 1997.

[13] Ted Schettler, Toxic Threats to Neurological Development of Children, Environmental Health Perspectives, Volume 109, Supplement 6, December 2001

[14] Tom Muir and Mike Zegarac, Societal Costs of Exposure to Toxic Substances, Environmental Health Perspectives, Volume 109, Supplement 6, December 2001.

[15] Paul S. Kibel, FAB Quarterly Viewpoint, Full Cleanup Preserves Full Value, www fablae.com/cleanup htm.; Mundy Associates, LLC, Contaminated Property: Issues and Answers, June 2002, www.mundyassoc.com/contaminated.htm.

There are also adverse economic affects and viability impacts on the communities inundated with brownfields, superfund, and other abandoned lands, especially when those sites are contaminated. In addition, these sites provide continued exposure to contamination. Though some funding opportunities exist via new initiatives for the communities with brownfields, the funding is limited and few receive these benefits. In addition, there is the cost of cleaning up these sites, which often become contaminated due to failed regulation and enforcement. The economic brunt for the cleanup of superfund sites is falling more on the taxpayers and less on the polluters.

In communities and indigenous lands throughout the country there exists subsistence farmers and fisherman who depend on the land to support their families food needs. Pollutants, especially PBTs that get into the food chain and heavy metals, can have devastating impacts on this way of life. In addition, those small community businesses such as fish farms that depend on the environmental health of the water and land are also negatively economically impacted.

In urban centers, abandoned lines or sites create blight furthering the economic decline of the surrounding area. Similarly, rural communities are impacted with reduced property value for large tracts of land, which may contribute to land loss, becomingly increasingly more impacted by the operation of large manufacturing facilities.

International Impacts

Pollution prevention has the potential to reduce pollution impacts on an international level. Globalization has resulted in the shifting of industrial production to developing countries along with accompanying pollution and adverse health-related effects.[16] Global warming due to fossil fuel use, increased use of pesticides, and exploitation of natural resources in Third World countries by multinational corporations causing loss of biodiversity, erosion and deforestation are all the results of unsustainable policies and practices that threaten the entire planet but could be reduced through pollution prevention measures.[17] Most developing countries also do not have environmental regulation. History shows that lack of environmental regulation enables industries that produce toxic waste to be less responsible in pollution prevention.

---

[16] Khabir Ahmed, <u>World Bank Predicts Development for the Next Century</u>, The Lancet, September 18, 1999; <u>Indoor Air Pollution Exposure Well Over WHO Guidelines</u>, Health & Medicine Week, October 2-October 9, 2000; Kenny Pronezuk, James Akre, Gerald Moy, Constanza Vallenas, <u>Global Perspectives in Breast Milk Contamination: Infectious and Toxic Hazards,</u> Environmental Health Perspectives, Volume 110, Number 6, June 2002.

[17] Joy Chen, Rachel Rivera, <u>A Pocket Guide to the Environmental Millennium</u>, The Amicus Journal, Volume 21, p. 22, January 2000; Richard Fenske, <u>Incorporating Health and Ecological Costs into Agricultural Production,</u> Environmental Health Perspectives, Volume 110, Number 5, May 2002.

ENFORCEMENT ISSUES

An essential component of a pollution prevention approach is compliance with existing environmental laws and regulations. From the perspective of communities, much of the adverse impacts that they experience would not occur if the regulatory agencies charged with environmental and public health protection were more effective in carrying out their statutory duties. Enforcement is often delegated by the US EPA to state regulatory agencies and some communities are concerned that their states have dysfunctional enforcement and compliance programs and that EPA does not exert their oversight responsibilities. It is believed that this dysfunction is both cultural and financial in nature. Pollution prevention strategies need to address both the cultural and financial.

Government actions to exempt farmwater PBT runoff from regulation as pollution,[18] to exempt burning of fields, to "grandfather" old and polluting facilities[19] such as coal burning power plants, proposals to reduce or abolish reporting requirements[20], declines in state inspections and enforcement,[21] and elimination or suspension of environmental rules[22] form the basis for the belief of some communities that governmental protection has not been as effective as is necessary to improve environmental quality.

Many communities consider the most egregious failure of environmental protection to be the acceptance and toleration of compliance challenged or "flagrant violators". These include industrial facilities that report or fail to report hundreds of tons of accidental releases, companies that operate without permits, and / or repeated permit violators, whose actions allow toxic releases to impact upon adjoining communities. Failure to clean up or restore contaminated areas, imposition of fines that have no deterrence effect and poor oversight of delegated programs by the Environmental Protection Agency are examples of enforcement failures by governments that should be providing oversight. These and other activities support legitimate complaints about the violator's negative environmental impact on environmental justice communities and to the quality of the environmental protection provided by regulatory agencies.

Equity in enforcement efforts is a matter of concern for low income communities and communities of color. Disproportionately impacted communities regularly report that areas with significant environmental problems rarely see a resolution of those problems

---

[18] Paul Rogers, California Environmentalists Want Farmers to Adhere to Clean Water Laws, San Jose Mercury News, February 22, 2002.

[19] Darren Samuelsohn, National Park Visibility Hinges on EPA Regs, Land Letter, June 27, 2002.

[20] Solid Waste Reporter, Activitists Say Public Health Threatened Under EPA Plan to Slash RCRA Regs, 2002; Sierra Club Environmental Quality Strategy Team, July 2002.

[21] Id.

[22] Arianna Huffington, What Are They Thinking In Washington?, Sierra Magazine, September-October 2002.

despite the efforts of government. The phenomenon of unequal environmental protection in communities of color and low-income communities has been documented in a growing body of research, including the National Law Journal's 1992 study on EPA's superfund program titled *"Separate but Unequal"* and Robert Bullard's book *Unequal Protection.*[23] Just one example of this failure of enforcement is found in the 1984 General Motors Superfund site adjoining the St. Regis Mohawk Reservation. A thirty-five foot high sludge pile of toxic waste has impacted contaminated fish, water and members of the tribe in the area for decades causing the Office of the New York Attorney General to threaten a lawsuit. According to the Attorney General's Office, "[t]hey have basically flouted the law for twenty five years".[24] Hopes that the EPA would step in and pressure the company to clean up the site never materialized.[25]

ADDRESSING COMMUNITY IMPACTS THROUGH POLLUTION PREVENTION

Implementing pollution prevention measures to achieve environmental justice is based upon accepting several underlying related philosophical premises. The first premise is the protection of human health and the environment, which are the chief goals of the environmental justice movement that can be achieved through pollution prevention. Another key goal is sustainable development, since this leads to societal and economic justice for environmental justice communities and the population at large. While other stakeholders may have additional goals, this is a goal of the Pollution Prevention Act and the federal and state environmental statutes and should be acknowledged as a key objective for the workgroup.

A second premise is that pollution prevention activities that result in improving environmental quality for communities can be achieved without sacrificing jobs, economic stability or environmental quality.[26] No one should have to choose between a clean, healthy environment and jobs. Resistance to new pollution prevention activities on the grounds that it threatens jobs must be exposed as an environmental myth and economic blackmail. By contrast evidence suggests that pollution prevention activities have the potential to create new employment opportunities in the manufacturing, transportation and utility industries.[27] Research by the Institute for Southern Studies

---

[23] Marianne Lavell & Marcia Coyle, A Special Report; Unequal Protection: The Racial Divide in Environmental Law, Nat'l L.J., Sept. 21, 1992; Robert D. Bullard, Unequal Protection: Environmental Justice & Communities of Color, 1994

[24] Somini Sengupta, A Sick Tribe and a Dump as a Neighbor, The New York Times, April 7, 2001.

[25] Id

[26] Alex Barnum, Environmental Study Disputes the Belief That Rules Cost Jobs and Stifle the Economy, The San Francisco Chronicle, March 19, 1996.

[27] Id.

ranking state economic performance with environmental measures has consistently found that the states that work to promote a healthy environment have sound economies.[28]

A third premise supporting the concept of pollution prevention as a way of improving advancing environmental justice and environmental quality is acknowledging the importance of enforcement. Enforcement is not a substitute for pollution prevention nor is pollution prevention a substitute for enforcement. Enforcement is necessary in the absence of compliance and often involves the imposition of fines or penalties intended to have a deterrent effect. Inadequate fines fail to achieve deterrence and lead to the conclusion that fines and penalties are a cost of doing business that can be absorbed.[29] Anecdotal evidence from the U.S. Department of Justice indicates that certain environmental programs which lack strong criminal sanctions (such as the mobile source requirements under the Clean Air Act) often have high rates of violation, suggesting that criminal sanctions create a deterrent effect.[30]

Pollution prevention must start from a baseline of compliance with existing local, state, Tribal and Federal environmental laws and better enforcement when needed. Increasing fines and penalties in the case of flagrant violations of environmental law is a mechanism available to reduce pollution and should be used when warranted. Pollution prevention should also include fully implementing the Pollution Prevention Act by identifying the opportunities in existing federal environmental laws for more fully incorporating pollution prevention.

A forth premise for implementing pollution prevention to achieve environmental justice affirms the relationship between pollution prevention and sustainable community development. A multifaceted approach to building grassroots capacity for pollution prevention strategizing and project implementation begins with a vision for a strong, healthy and sustainable community. Community development organizations must include pollution prevention as a requirement for community planning and project development. Planning for a thriving, productive, healthy community is a proactive approach to restoring communities and safeguarding them from future damage.

A fifth premise for incorporating pollution prevention as an environmental justice strategy is the recognition that pollution prevention measures must address the needs of special populations. Children, the elderly, individuals with compromised immune systems, women of child-bearing ages and other susceptible populations must be considered when developing measures to reduce pollution. Cumulative impacts must also be addressed.

---

[28] Mark Douglas Whitaker, Green and Gold 2000, Institute for Southern Studies, November 2000, www.southernstudies.org

[29] Sharon Begley and Bob Cohn, One Deal That Was Too Good for Exxon, Newsweek, May 6, 1991.

[30] Suellen Keiner, Esq., Forum on Deterence of Environmental Violations and Environmental Crime, Environmental Law Institute, July 1999

In order to make a significant difference in environmental quality a final premise is that opportunities and areas for incorporating pollution prevention to advance environmental justice currently exist. These are areas where pollution prevention can make a huge difference now in the lives of low-income communities and communities of color.

AREAS WHERE POLLUTION PREVENTION CAN IMPROVE ENVIRONMENTAL QUALITY

Pollution prevention technologies can reduce the impacts of fugitive emissions from stationary sources. Integrated pest management can reduce health and other pollution impacts to farmworkers from pesticides and agricultural chemicals using source reduction, process changes and product substitution. Dry cleaners, printers and metal shops have all been involved in pollution prevention measures that involved source reduction, product substitution and production or process changes. Auto repair facilities have been successfully involved in a number of pollution prevention initiatives to reduce exposures through best management practices.

In the beauty care field, beauticians and customers in a Boston community concerned about toxic exposure to chemicals in hairdressing solons focusing on hair straighteners and artificial nails products came up with an idea for healthy hair shows using environmentally sound hair using nontoxic hair care products. A Massachusetts beauty school developed a curriculum for teachers and students to identify chemical hazards, choose less toxic alternatives and incorporate pollution prevention including source reduction into their daily practices.[31] In the service field janitors and other service workers can benefit from pollution prevention by reducing exposure and toxicity in the cleaning products they use.[32] The California Basket Weavers Association is working to preserve traditional California Indian basketweaving culture by pressuring the Forest Service to reduce pesticide use on forestlands.[33] Transportation impacts from emissions of diesel fuel by trucks, buses and other vehicles affect most urban communities in the United States. Transportation impacts can be reduced through the use of alternative fuels and cleaner technologies.[34]

For larger industrial manufacturing facilities toxic pollutants raise concerns because sources of emissions and people are concentrated in the same geographic area, leading to large numbers of people exposed to the emissions of many hazardous air pollutants.

---

[31] Massachusetts Toxic Use Reduction Institute, Community Toxic Use Reduction Program, Community Education Program, Health and Beauty Go Hand in Hand: TUR in the Putnam Vocational Cosmetology Department and Healthy Hair Campaign to Reduce the Use of Toxics in Neighbprhood Hari Salons,(2001) available at http://208.56.92.121/community/smallbusiness/health_hair.shtml, Interview with Ken Gieser.

[32] Inform, Cleaning for Health: Products and Practices for a Safer Indoor Environment (2002)

[33] California Basket Weavers Association, P.O. Box 2397, Nevada City, California 95959 (2000).

[34] National Alternative Fuels Day and Environmental Summit, Summary of Outcomes and Recommendations, Hostos Community College, Bronx, New York (April 2002).

Emissions from older facilities, especially coal-burning power plants, are especially troublesome as they contribute tons of pollutants annually and are either not bound by regulations, or those regulations are not being enforced. In order to maintain standard of living while protecting human health and the environment, fundamental changes are required in the area of product and process substitution, focusing on the design of chemical products and processes that reduce or eliminate the use and generation of hazardous substances. Human health and environmental benefits can be realized by designing toxicity and hazard out of the chemical manufacturing process. Pollution prevention should target local sources with effective solutions. The potential through these efforts is enormous. More than 113 million lbs/yr (56,500 tons/yr) of hazardous chemicals and more than 152 million lbs (76,000 tons to date) of solvents have been eliminated through Green Chemistry initiatives. This includes elimination of CFC and VOC solvents as well as persistent, toxic, and bioaccumulative (PBT) chemicals. These programs have also saved 55 million gallons/yr of water, saved 88.9 trillion BTU/yr of energy, and eliminated 57 million lbs/yr of carbon dioxide emissions.[35] Recycling and reuse initiatives should also not be downplayed. Though not defined as pollution prevention in EPA's definition, nevertheless these activities have reduced amount of waste in landfills and promoted programs where the entire community participated.

There have been a variety of initiatives to promote product and process substitution in low-income communities and communities of color. Programs involving waste minimization, recycling, reuse and sustainable development are all classic examples of how pollution prevention can be used in environmental justice communities to bring about positive change. These are just a few of the areas where pollution prevention can advance environmental justice but many other opportunities to implement pollution prevention exist and the ways that pollution prevention can be helpful are only limited by the imagination.

CAPACITY-BUILDING FOR EFFECTIVE COMMUNITY PARTICIPATION IN POLLUTION PREVENTION

Building community capacity to improve incorporation of pollution prevention activities, tools and activities into community advocacy strategies requires a concerted effort. Communities must be included at the outset in government and local facilities pollution prevention planning activities in order to help identify priorities and measure progress. In order for communities to participate affectively and on a level playing field, resource and training needs must be addressed. Communities must have adequate information with respect to permit limitations and permit noncompliance, emissions, discharges, accidental releases, on site treatment, storage and disposal, to name a few. Government and industry in order to facilitate cooperation and build trust should freely share this information. Despite recent trends to reduce environmental information available on

---

[35] Mary Kirchhoff, The Green Chemistry Institute.

EPA's website and from regulatory agencies, security concerns must be balanced with the need for communities to know what toxins are present in their environment in order for communities to assist in the development of effective strategies to reduce exposures.

In order for communities to participate in pollution prevention activities, there must be adequate and sustained funding from public and private sources to support their efforts. There should also be funding, tax incentives or subsidies to develop clean production technologies and to directly support community-driven environmental justice, pollution prevention and sustainable development projects. Educational materials suitable for the layman must be developed and comprehensive educational training initiatives should be undertaken. Community participation must be valued and that value should be demonstrated with support and respect for their involvement. Governmental technical assistance and resources to enable communities to hire independent technical assistance is also necessary to build the capacity of communities to effectively participate in advancing pollution prevention as an environmental justice tool.

COMMUNITY RECOMMENDATIONS

There are many opportunities in existing environmental laws to incorporate pollution prevention. The Pollution Prevention Act mandates the development and implementation of strategies to promote source reduction. Other federal environmental statutes also require pollution prevention activities, offer opportunities to incorporate pollution prevention into permits or include resource conservation directives. The current EPA Administrator has committed to integrating environmental justice into existing environmental statutes. This provides a statutory opportunity to employ pollution prevention approaches in environmental justice communities. In addition to these opportunities, the community stakeholder representatives has the following recommendations:

1. Community involvement is the bedrock to any pollution prevention strategy in impacted communities. Models for engaging the public in order to maximize their involvement are crucial in ensuring that the community will be engaged.
2. A collection of case studies with viable examples featuring community participation and community driven pollution prevention collaborations would be useful as an example of successful pollution prevention partnerships. A clearinghouse with the case studies could be placed on a website and a toolkit could be developed and provided to local governments and community organizations detailing the steps to an effective community involvement process in pollution prevention projects.
3. The Environmental Justice and Pollution Prevention Grants should be made available again. Successful projects developed through that program should receive sustained funding and expanded to other environmental justice communities, thereby building on the success.

4. Pollution prevention resources and funds should be directed primarily at impacted communities and their selected representatives which are addressing environmental justice and pollution prevention issues, not other external bodies such as organizations set up by polluters.

5. Increase community awareness. Diesel education project were effective in terms of level of awareness. Dry cleaner project raised awareness.

6. A national disease registry, beyond cancer, of diseases associated with chemical releases should be established. This registry should monitor disease associated with chemicals being released should exposure occur and develop innovative responses to reduce it. Most states have cancer registries or lead poisoning registries and several states have legislation calling for epidemiological research into the prevention of environmentally related diseases. Disease registries and especially lead poisoning registries have resulted in reductions of lead exposures to children as areas of disproportionate lead exposure are identified.

7. The environmental justice community strongly recommends that the precautionary principle be incorporated in environmental decision-making and the development of environmental regulations, policy and programs particularly in over-burdened communities (exposure to cumulative and synergistic affects).

8. Incentives should be developed that encourage businesses to employ a precautionary approach in their production processes.

9. A variety of improved enforcement mechanisms can serve as effective pollution prevention tools in appropriate cases including increased use of Supplemental Environmental Projects that focus on pollution prevention.

10. Fines and penalties imposed for noncompliance should be set aside to fund environmental initiatives for the burdened community. There is precedent for this and it serves as a way to assure that local benefits result from the imposition of fines.

11. Better oversight by EPA and review of delegated programs should be employed to improve enforcement measures in cases of environmental protection failures. At the same time, governmental efficiency can be improved by streamlining bureaucracy unless public health or the environment is imperiled.

12. Brownfield projects should focus on green building, green business and green industry incubation models.

13. Restoration of on and off-site areas impacted by pollution should be accomplished using sustainable remediation practices such as photo-remediation.

14. Where cumulative impacts are apparent, a pollution reduction plan should be developed with the help of the federal government and should be memorialized in an enforceable agreement even if the surrounding facilities operate within the legal limits. The federal agency should also provide resources to the local government to assist in the plan.

15. Small businesses and entrepreneurial enterprises should receive technical assistance and support if they are willing to incorporate pollution prevention in their business philosophy and practices. Communities that are heavily

71

industrialized are in a position to gain tremendous environmental benefits by receiving this type of stimulation for small businesses.

16. Pollution prevention activities should support and promote renewable energy options for small businesses and communities.

17. Additional support for alternative fuel projects should be focused in impacted communities.

18. In areas where Clear Skies projections indicate that non-attainment for ozone will exist for the foreseeable future, aggressive pollution prevention conditions should be imposed in new and renewal air permits.

19. There is an effort to bring back old power plants in communities of color. Convert dirty power plants to new clean/green ones and use clean air alternatives. If plants cannot be converted, they should be shut down.

20. Pollution prevention should be used as a proactive opportunity to advance environmental stewardship values in impacted communities.

21. Pollution prevention should focus on reducing the number of chemicals and minimization of persistent, bioaccumulative, toxic (PBT) chemicals.

22. Reduce amounts of pesticides used and increase research on and support models for sustainable agriculture (organic).

23. Funds should actually get to grass roots organizations and not organizations set up by polluters. Organizations with exemplary records should get the funds.

24. Performance track award criteria should include environmental justice measures.

25. Build a pollution prevention assessment model that is holistic. This model will educate communities and provide assessment capabilities by making linkages between the environmental issue and the social / developmental issue. For example, air quality and the associated respiratory problem for seniors in the community was helpful. Linking lead poisoning to birth defects helped get expected mothers involved. Ties to religion and a responsibility to environmental justice also helped get the church involved.

26. Move from diesel and get buses converted to natural gases and three-minute idling law.

CONCLUSION

Pollution prevention, as defined by the act, incorporates protection of public health and the environment, including protecting environmental resources for subsequent generations, as key values. These are also key values of the environmental justice movement. Pollution prevention provides a unique opportunity for communities, business and government to work together in a non-confrontational way to achieve some joint aims. Communities' are in support of providing resources for the development and implementation of clean technologies to business. Businesses support the concept of reducing the impact of their activities on surrounding communities. Government supports the reduction of pollution impacts on public health and the environment. These shared values offer the potential for the stakeholders to work collaboratively in a way that may not have been available to them previously, to develop innovative strategies that meet their interests that do not require enforcement, to build trust and improve communications in their relationships, and to work together towards the goal of achieving environmental justice.

ADVANCING ENVIRONMENTAL JUSTICE THROUGH POLLUTION PREVENTION
NEJAC Pollution Prevention Report
June 2003

CHAPTER 4: TRIBAL PERSPECTIVES

This chapter was authored by members of the Tribal Stakeholder group to elaborate on the views of the members of that group, not necessarily reflect the views of members of other stakeholder groups or of the NEJAC Executive Council.

THE LEGAL STATUS AND RIGHTS OF TRIBES

For tribes pollution prevention concerns and possible approaches for implementing pollution prevention must be considered in the complex context of the unique position of tribes in American society. American Indian and Alaska Native Tribes are sovereign governments recognized as self-governing under federal law. As such they are entitled to make and enforce laws on their lands and to create governmental entities such as courts. In addition, the federal government has a trust responsibility to tribes whereby the federal government has charged itself with moral obligations to tribes of a fiduciary nature requiring it to ensure the protection of tribal interests.[1] This trust responsibility is predicated, in part, upon more than 400 treaties through which tribes ceded vast portions of their aboriginal lands in exchange for the federal government's solemn promise to protect the rights of tribes to exist as self-governing nations.[2] The trust responsibility is also based on acts of Congress, Executive Orders and federal court decisions.[3] The trust doctrine reflects the fact that the federal government holds legal title to most Indian land in trust for the tribes (or for individual Indian landowners) and, consequently, has the duties of a trustee to manage natural resources for the benefit of tribes. The trust doctrine also includes the responsibility to protect and support tribal sovereignty.[4] The relationship between the United States and tribes is often described as "government-to-government," which reflects the fact that tribes are sovereigns. This relationship is different from the relationship between the federal government and the states, in part because of the federal trust responsibility to the tribes.

The status of Alaska Native tribes is different from those in the "lower forty-eight" because, with one exception, Alaska Native tribes do not have "reservations" and the federal government does not hold their lands in trust.[5] The federal government nevertheless has a trust responsibility to these tribes as well, and they are recognized as possessing some aspects of sovereignty.

---

[1] National Environmental Justice Advisory Council, Indigenous Peoples Subcommittee, <u>Guide on Consultation and Collaboration with Indian Tribal Governments and The Public Participation of Indigenous Groups and Tribal Members in Environmental Decision Making</u>, November 2000

[2] Id. at p. 9.

[3] *See generally* FELIX S. COHEN, HANDBOOK OF FEDERAL INDIAN LAW 220-228 (1982 ed.)

[4] 25 U.S.C. §3601 (recognizing that "the United States has a trust responsibility to each tribal government that includes the protection of the sovereignty of each tribal government").

[5] <u>See generally</u> Cohen, *supra* note 3, at 739-70.

The federal government has not always lived up to its obligations to Indian tribes. In contemporary America, many Indian tribes live with the legacy of the "allotment" era of 1887 to 1934, when federal laws sought to force Indian people to give up their tribal ways of life and become assimilated into the mainstream of American society. During the allotment era, the federal government forcibly took commonly owned lands from many tribes, allotted these lands to individual tribal members (generally to encourage farming), and invited non-Indians to settle on the so-called "surplus" lands.[6] Congress repudiated the policies of the allotment era in 1934, but the legacy is that many reservations have substantial populations of non-Indians, many of whom are landowners. In the last quarter century, although Congress and the Executive Branch have consistently supported tribal self-government, the Supreme Court has imposed new limits on the sovereign powers of tribal governments, in effect resurrecting the repudiated policies of the allotment era.[7]

Some indigenous communities are not currently recognized as sovereigns by the federal government, but such communities may nonetheless have environmental or public health concerns that are different from other groups or the general public due to a subsistence lifestyle or unique cultural practices.[8] As citizens of the United States, indigenous groups or organizations and individual members of recognized tribes also have the rights to environmental and public health protection from federal agencies available to other citizens.[9]

Federal agencies must interact with tribes in a manner consistent with their sovereign status and rights under federal law. To accomplish this aim, the Environmental Protection Agency has adopted a formal policy statement governing its relationship with tribes and the implementation of its programs on Indian reservations.[10] EPA's policy states that EPA will incorporate Indian Policy goals into its planning and management activities including, among other things, its budget, legislative initiatives and management accountability system.[11] Beginning in 1986, several of the major federal environmental statutes have been amended to authorize EPA to treat tribes like states for various purposes, and EPA has issued numerous sets of regulations to carry out these

---

[6] See generally Id. at 127-39.

[7] See generally David H. Getches, Conquering the Cultural Frontier: The New Subjectivism of the Supreme Court in Indian Law, 84 CAL. L. REV. 1573 (1996); Philip P. Frickey, A Common Law for Our Age of Colonialism: The Judicial Divestiture of Indian Tribal Authority Over Nonmembers, 109 YALE L. J. 1 (1999).

[8] National Environmental Justice Advisory Council, Indigenous Peoples Subcommittee, Guide on Consultation and Collaboration with Indian Tribal Governments and The Public Participation of Indigenous Groups and Tribal Members in Environmental Decision Making, November 2000 at p. 10.

[9] Id.

[10] Environmental Protection Agency, American Indian Environmental Office, EPA Policy for the Administration of Environmental Programs on Indian Reservations, 1984, www.epa.gov/indian/1984 htm.

[11] Id

statutory amendments. Many tribes have made substantial progress in developing environmental regulatory programs pursuant to federal law, but many obstacles have proven difficult to overcome. Some obstacles are matters of funding and other kinds of assistance; other obstacles have to do with challenges to the exercise of tribal sovereign powers. The result is that in much of Indian the environmental regulatory infrastructure is simply not comparable to that in most of America.

TRIBAL POLLUTION CONCERNS THAT CAN BE ADDRESSED BY POLLUTION PREVENTION

Tribal pollution prevention concerns can be categorized by a variety of owner-operator interests. Pollution may be generated by nongovernmental entities, by tribal members, by nonmember Indians, by non-Indians, by corporate and business entities and by small businesses that may be tribal operating on tribal trust lands, on individually-owned Indian trust lands, or on private lands within reservation boundaries.

The tribal entities with the authority to address these pollution prevention concerns include the legislative and executive branches of tribal governments, tribal government agencies and departments and tribal business enterprises. Federal agencies, acting in a manner consistent with their trust responsibilities, also have the authority to implement pollution prevention measures in the context of their land management or financial assistance roles. These agencies include, the Bureau of Indian Affairs, the National Park Service, the Fish and Wildlife Service, and the Indian Health Service, Department Housing Development, and the Administration for Native Americans. Some agencies manage lands outside reservation boundaries (and in some cases within reservation boundaries) where pollution prevention measures could benefit reservation environments or off-reservation resources in which tribes have treaty or statutory rights or other interests. Such agencies include the Bureau of Land Management, the National Park Service, Fish and Wildlife Service, Forest Service, and the Department of Defense. Each agency responsible for generating pollution on Indian lands, or affecting off-reservation resources of importance to tribes, should have a fully funded viable pollution prevention program in place that was developed in consultation with tribes.

State and local agencies including municipalities also have the ability to address pollution concerns through pollution prevention measures in consultation with tribes. Nonfederal projects on tribal lands that are permitted or funded cause additional pollution impacts.

Pollution concerns of some tribes, particularly those with reservations near international boundaries, may also be addressed by entities that have transboundary authority such as the International Joint Commission which oversees water quantity and quality in the rivers and lakes that lie along or flow across the United States-Canada Border,[12] the Commission for Environmental Cooperation which studies and makes recommendations on the long range transport of air pollution, the International Air Quality Advisory Board,[13] the United Nations Economic Commission for Europe,[14] Environment Canada or Partners in Flight which oversees populations of migratory birds and others. There are wide ranges of pollution generating activities that take place on tribal lands and each activity creates different adverse environmental impacts. These activities include mineral extraction, agriculture, forestry, waste disposal, and storage and processing activities, industrial plants, schools, federal and tribal governmental facilities and infrastructure and Department of Defense facilities.

These activities result in numerous adverse environmental impacts. For example mineral extraction is extremely damaging and causes air, water and soil pollution. Agriculture and forestry causes soil and water pollution and results in habitat loss and loss of biodiversity, wildlife and marine life. Waste storage, disposal and processing may cause air, soil and water pollution. Operation of industrial plants, schools, and federal and tribal governmental facilities may result in air, water and soil pollution as well as impacts upon cultural resources, cultural practices and sacred sites. Finally Department of Defense facilities have had devastating pollution impacts on tribal lands including impacts on air, water and soil. All of these polluting activities can have adverse impacts on historical resources. All of these activities have adverse impacts on human environmental and ecological health.

In many ways, environmental health impacts on tribal lands are similar to health impacts for other low-income communities and communities of color. These health impacts include asthma, diabetes, hypertension, thyroid disorders, cancer and leukemia. Some impacts may be different, for example because of higher levels of fish consumption or because of other kinds of cultural practices that are rooted in the environment. Impacts may also be different because impacts on culturally important environmental resources may be manifested in psychological suffering in people.

Issues of geography affect pollution concerns of tribes. These are impacts on the reservations from sources on tribal lands, impacts on tribal lands or cross boundary impacts from sources off the reservations and pollution that occurs outside of the reservations that have impacts on off reservation resources.

---

[12] Canadian Department of Foreign Affairs and International Trade, The Environment Has No Borders, Water Quality/Quantity, www.can-am.gc.ca/menu-e.asp?mid+1&cat=11.

[13] International Air Quality Advisory Board, Special Report on Transboundary Air Quality Issues, November 1998, www.ijc.org/boards/iaqab/spectrans/chap7 html.

[14] Id.

ADVANCING ENVIRONMENTAL JUSTICE THROUGH POLLUTION PREVENTION
NEJAC Pollution Prevention Report
June 2003

There are also pollution prevention issues that are peculiar to tribes. One of these issues is structural inequity in the enforcement of environmental laws.

Environmental law is carried out through "cooperative federalism" between the federal government and the states, and Indian reservations were left out of this cooperation during the first two decades that state programs were being developed. Inadequate funding for tribal programs is considered by many to be an environmental justice issue and an impediment to effective consultation with tribes due to the limited capacity of many tribal environmental programs.[15] Inequity in technical assistance and federal grant support for tribal environmental and pollution prevention development and implementation in comparison to states is an important environmental and pollution prevention issue for tribes.

Pollution exposures and the need for pollution prevention may be greater for some reservation communities due to the nature of polluting activities that occur on tribal lands. On some reservations, there is a higher level of natural resource development that occurs within tribal lands. These activities include mining, and oil and gas extraction and refining. Many tribes, including many Alaska Native tribes, are also adversely affected by polluting activities beyond the reach of their territorial jurisdiction.

In the case of facilities owned or managed by tribal governments that are not in compliance with federal environmental statutes, EPA will not take direct action through judicial or administrative process unless EPA determines that there is a significant threat to human health or the environment, EPA action could be expected to achieve effective results in a timely manner, and the federal government cannot utilize other alternatives to correct the problem in a timely fashion.[16] In cases where facilities are owned or managed by private parties with no substantial tribal interest or control, the agency will endeavor to work in cooperation with the affected tribal government but will otherwise respond to noncompliance by private parties on Indian reservations as the agency would to noncompliance by the private sector elsewhere in the country.[17] Another issue that effects pollution prevention for tribes is limits on tribal sovereignty imposed by the United States Supreme Court.[18] According to holdings of the Supreme Court, tribal sovereignty is not absolute; rather, aspects of the original sovereignty of the tribes may have been given up in a treaty, taken away by Congress or divested by implication as a result of their dependent status.[19] As a result, the authority to undertake pollution prevention measures may be subject to limits that are not imposed on other governments.

---

[15] EPA Policy for the Administration of Environmental Programs on Indian Reservations, supra note 10.
[16] Id.
[17] Guide, supra note 1 at p. 7.
[18] Id.
[19] See generally.Getches and Frickey, supra note 7.

From the perspective of tribes, the limitations of conventional risk assessment methods are another issue unique to tribes. Tribal cultural and spiritual values are not adequately considered in traditional risk assessment processes. Accordingly, many tribes, and the environmental professionals who work for them regard risk assessment as a tool that has little value.

POSSIBLE APPROACHES FOR IMPLEMENTING POLLUTION PREVENTION IN AND NEAR TRIBAL LANDS

Governmental action is a key component necessary for implementing effective pollution prevention activities for tribes.

In keeping with its Indian policy and the trust responsibility, EPA should take steps, in consultation with tribes, to fill the enforcement gaps in Indian country and Native Alaska. The expanded use of Direct Implementation of Tribal Cooperative Agreements ("DITCAs") is one approach. In addition, EPA, possibly in cooperation with other federal agencies, could provide assistance to tribes for the development of Tribal Environmental Policy Acts ("TEPAs") that include pollution prevention requirements. Land use planning under tribal law to promote pollution prevention is another approach to advance pollution prevention activities on tribal lands. This could include promoting walkable neighborhoods, incorporating smart growth principles, using geographic information system technologies to assist in land use analysis and planning and including tribal departments involved in planning activities such as tribal housing authorities. Supreme Court case law, however, renders it difficult for tribes to implement comprehensive land use planning on lands that are not held in federal trust status.

The precautionary principle is an important pollution prevention measure, and many people have noted that this principle is generally consistent with tribal cultural values. Tribal laws that stress the precautionary principle could advance pollution prevention on tribal lands as issues of uncertainty are resolved in favor of protection of public health, the environment and concern for the seventh generation.

Pollution prevention education programs are also needed to advance pollution prevention in and near tribal lands. This includes education programs for tribal officials and staff and for the general public on the reservations, for small businesses, for farmers, and for youth. Development and implementation of environmental programs requires increases in federal support for technical assistance, funding for development and implementation of tribal pollution prevention programs and tribal environmental program infrastructure.

For pollution prevention to be effective it must be supported at the highest levels of government. This means that for tribes there must also be pollution prevention leadership development and training provided to tribal leaders, and included in tribal programs such

ADVANCING ENVIRONMENTAL JUSTICE THROUGH POLLUTION PREVENTION
NEJAC Pollution Prevention Report
June 2003

as to the tribal natural resources, environment, housing, education, economic development and planning departments and to members of the tribal public.

Tribal governments may be able to show leadership in developing and supporting initiatives in pollution prevention for small businesses and industries operating within reservation boundaries. Similarly, when facilities are operating outside of reservation boundaries but causing cross-boundary impacts, or causing impact of off-reservation resources of importance to tribes, tribal governments could pursue the development of memorandum of understandings ("MOU") with adjoining governmental entities such as states or municipalities. Such MOUs might also be generally helpful in addressing pollution prevention issues and implementing pollution prevention programs.

Actions by the federal government would also be extremely useful in advancing pollution prevention in and near tribal lands. The federal government should undertake outreach to tribes to assure that they are included in technical assistance to nonfederal governments. EPA and other federal agencies should also devote more attention and resources to their consultations with tribes in the context of proposed actions that are subject to the National Environmental Policy Act or National Historic Preservation Act, for actions that would result in affects within reservation boundaries, on no-reservation tribal communities, and on off-reservation resources of importance to tribes.

In order to advance pollution prevention on tribal lands, federal agencies should provide increased and sustained support for technical assistance and funding for pollution prevention and tribal environmental program development and implementation. The federal government should provide support for pollution prevention leadership development and training to elected tribal leaders and to tribal programs. Support from the federal government should be available to incorporate pollution prevention into the operations of tribal natural resource, environment, housing, education, economic development and planning departments. There should also be federal support provided for pollution prevention training provided to members of the tribal public and non-Indian residents of tribal lands. Federal agencies should assist in supporting tribal government initiatives in pollution prevention for small businesses and industries operating on tribal lands. Resources in the form of grants should be made available to schools, community-based tribal organizations and non-governmental entities for pollution prevention initiatives and activities.

State and local governments should be encouraged to work collaboratively with tribal governments and entities to implement pollution prevention activities within or near reservations and other tribal communities. State and local governments should identify potentially concerned tribal governments in the initial stages of any state or local initiatives involving pollution prevention and seek to engage such tribes in consultation and collaboration. When such efforts result in genuine collaboration, states and local

ADVANCING ENVIRONMENTAL JUSTICE THROUGH POLLUTION PREVENTION
NEJAC Pollution Prevention Report
June 2003

governments should enter into cooperative agreements with tribes such as MOUs, MOA and other contractual agreements, in order to seal such agreements.

In recognition of the cultural values of tribes, states and local governments should endeavor to incorporate the precautionary principle into any initiatives that affect resources that are important to tribes. Similarly, educational programs involving pollution prevention developed and implemented by states and local governments should include outreach to and participation from tribal governments, departments, and schools, as well as community-based organizations and other nongovernmental entities.

Finally, nongovernmental entities operating on or near tribal lands should engage in best practices designed to reduce, to the greatest extent possible, adverse environmental and public health impacts on those lands. The same should apply to resources. Such entities should consider voluntarily agree to comply with tribal laws respecting pollution and memorialize those agreements in writing.

Respect for the sovereignty, values, history and cultural practices of American Indian and Alaska Native Tribes and the laws, treaties, policies and Executive Orders governing relationships with the tribes is instrumental for reducing pollution on or near tribal resources.

CHAPTER 5: BUSINESS & INDUSTRY PERSPECTIVES

This chapter was authored by members of the Business and Industry Stakeholder group to elaborate on the views of the members of that group, not necessarily reflect the views of members of other stakeholder groups or of the NEJAC Executive Council.

INTRODUCTION

Business and industry's perspectives on pollution prevention have several premises in common with other stakeholders. First, business agrees that the term is broad and can usefully encompass a variety of practices that may result in improved environmental performance. Second, the term represents environmental protection that at least meets or may exceed the baseline represented by traditional command and control environmental regulatory requirements. Pollution prevention activities encompass means to achieve numerical performance goals more reliably and efficiently; reductions in emissions beyond regulatory targets; holistic approaches to environmental quality (e.g., reducing pollutants that may not have current regulatory standards), and methods to promote sustainable use of resources. Pollution prevention frequently involves all levels of the business organization in designing approaches to minimize the impact of operations on human health and the environment. Finally, the term "pollution prevention" assumes communication and collaborative engagement with the members of the public.

In other respects, business and industry's positions on pollution prevention may differ from those of other stakeholders, or even individual members of other stakeholder groups. Operating under the premise that "the perfect is often the enemy of the good," the business community in general does not hold successful pollution prevention efforts to the criteria that they eliminate pollution, only that they reduce environmental and health impacts below the baseline of applicable regulatory standards. Although some companies have committed publicly to a zero emissions goal, for even those companies that goal is targeted for some time in the future. Moreover, it is fair to say that the majority of the business community does not consider a zero-emissions goal practical, or even feasible. The majority of companies believe that it is the express obligation of government-based environmental and health programs to assure that the levels of pollution allowable under regulatory programs protect, consistent with sound science and with an adequate margin of safety, all members of the community and the environment as a whole. For the majority of companies, some level of risk is perceived to be inherent in all human activities; the issue is whether this risk is reasonable and consistent with good health and environmental quality.

Despite their divergent perspectives, stakeholder groups may be able to forge sufficient agreement on areas of implementation of pollution prevention to improve meaningfully environmental conditions within communities. Depending on the regulatory, public relations, economic and other incentives, businesses may devote resources toward invention, innovation or adoption of new technologies that can reduce or eliminate pollution and save costs, or alternatively utilize well-established but less innovative techniques to satisfy rigid regulatory prescriptions. If communities can be assured that affording increased flexibility to businesses will yield enhanced environmental performance, particularly in the aspects of most concern to community members, pollution prevention may produce tangible benefits for both businesses and communities.

Business statements on pollution prevention make clear that, for the most part, such efforts, if they are to be sustainable and effective, must be voluntary rather than prescribed by regulation. In 1998, The Business Roundtable published a benchmarking study of pollution prevention planning among the Fortune 250 companies the association represents, and three conclusions were drawn:

- Pollution prevention planning will be important for years to come.

- Pollution prevention planning should be tailored to an organization's unique needs and circumstances – wherever possible, integrated into core business activities.

- Pollution prevention planning practices do not lend themselves to a "one size fits all" approach. Mandates can be beneficial in some circumstances but are detrimental in others.

"A Benchmarking Study of Pollution Prevention Planning: Best Practices, Issues, and Implications for Public Policy" (August 1998).

The third bullet is worth explaining. In the study, the Roundtable found that state-level pollution planning requirements were useful in giving a planning framework for companies unfamiliar with pollution prevention. For companies already participating in pollution reduction planning, however, these state-mandated paperwork requirements were duplicative of company practices and in some cases actually discouraged innovation, development of substantial new initiatives, and integration of pollution prevention planning into core business strategy. In effect, pollution prevention required by regulation became a paperwork exercise relegated to environmental, health and safety managers rather than an element of senior management's strategic design and operating plans. A well-designed government program would provide planning, education and assistance to less sophisticated companies while affording all companies the flexibility to implement pollution prevention strategies in innovative ways best suited to their organizations and cultures.

Business and industry's pollution prevention efforts routinely include public participation elements intended to communicate to the general public and to communities in which they operate company initiatives to improve environmental quality. For example,

84

pollution prevention efforts undertaken under EPA's Common Sense Initiative and Project XL include substantial dialogue and collaboration among facilities, regulators and community members on how changes to operations can reduce pollution while avoiding particular regulatory impediments. Precise and extensive public reporting of pollution prevention initiatives are part of the corporate environmental reports advocated by such groups as the Conference Board, the Global Environmental Management Initiative (GEMI), and the United Nations Environmental Program's (UNEP) Sustainability projects, as well as industry pollution prevention initiatives such as the chemical industry's 33/50 program. Brownfield projects, which by their nature voluntarily reduce pollution by remediating and reusing formerly impacted properties, routinely incorporate dialogue with neighboring community members to identify their goals for site response and reuse, whether these projects are coordinated by EPA, states or performed independently under the ASTM standard for brownfields.

The business literature on pollution prevention thus far has not focused on the opportunity to address environmental concerns in environmental justice communities in particular, but this focus could be a natural one. The broad-based organization called the Business Network for Environmental Justice, for example, was formed to engage constructively on means by which business and industry can successfully respond to environmental justice community concerns. Many existing environmental projects, although not developed with environmental justice in mind, actually provide benefits to communities of color and low-income populations. What has been lacking – and this report can begin to provide – is education on the ways in which targeted pollution prevention efforts can address the environmental quality concerns of environmental justice communities. To accompany this educational effort and to the extent resources and opportunities are available, it would be particularly important to create tangible incentives for business and industry to direct their pollution prevention efforts to such communities.

Many groups can participate in this education and response effort. For example, EPA and state-level pollution prevention programs and outreach efforts could target environmental justice communities in their literature, as part of their discussions with facilities in permitting and other proceedings, in their standard-setting activities and as part of their technical support in compliance assistance efforts. Groups supporting corporate environmental reporting (GEMI, the Conference Board, UNEP, ISO) could encourage separate line-item reporting on pollution prevention in environmental justice communities. Industry sectors with extensive community outreach programs like the chemical industry's Responsible Care and other "good neighbor" policies could focus on pollution prevention initiatives for environmental justice communities. They also could make consideration of the affected populations an element of audits and other environmental management techniques. Brownfields redevelopments could be tracked to identify where these efforts have lead to pollution reduction in environmental justice communities and brownfields grants targeted to these communities. Pollution prevention techniques could be considered in lieu of potentially less reliable end-of-pipe controls as

85

means of satisfying performance standards. Most effectively, regulatory and economic incentives and public recognition opportunities could be created to incentivize pollution prevention initiatives in environmental justice communities. EPA appropriations, or regulatory reform and streamlining efforts, could specifically reward business and industry voluntarily reducing pollution, conserving energy or using cleaner renewable energy sources, or using cleaner technology in environmental justice communities.

The following chapter attempts to lay the groundwork for the education and response outlined in the previous paragraph by describing an array of current business and industry efforts to prevent pollution. The chapter then suggests the resources, incentives and capacity building that should be undertaken to foster greater pollution prevention in environmental justice communities. Note that although this chapter focuses on efforts by business and industry, the projects, opportunities and expectations should be the same for comparable facilities operated by federal, state or local governments. Fueling stations owned by the Department of Defense or Interior, municipal waste trucks or disposal sites owned by municipalities, publicly owned treatment works and all other public sector facilities and activities owned or operated by the government organizations have equal incentives and obligations to seek out opportunities to prevent pollution, particularly in environmental justice communities. Likewise, non-profits such as educational institutions, hospitals and other organizations should be encompassed within the suggested pollution prevention approach.

This discussion focuses primarily on experiences by large and medium sized businesses, in some part because the literature of pollution prevention is written primarily about larger sources. Increasingly, focus is being placed on the continuing viability of small and mid-sized manufacturers (SMMs). The 307,000 U.S. SMMs produce more than half of the nation's manufacturing output and account for more than two-thirds of employment in the manufacturing sector. SMMs have specific challenges with regard to pollution prevention. The central issue should be how to induce SMMSs to invest in pollution prevention approaches that ultimately result in higher levels of quality and environmental performance and, in turn, lead to greater productivity and profit gain. SMMs are often less integrated into large trade associations that are capable of performing the research to develop pollution prevention techniques, and the competitive atmosphere in which SMMs operate makes the cost of pollution prevention a significant impediment. In many cases, the infrastructure for pollution prevention is particularly challenged if the sources are not subject to environmental permitting requirements that define a "safe" level of operations and create a baseline from which to identify pollution prevention opportunities. Moreover, without being actively engaged with EPA, an SSM is less likely to be informed of or adopt pollution prevention techniques or reach out to community members in a dialogue on environmental controls that a permitting process naturally affords. This lack of infrastructure can be particularly significant in urban environmental justice communities perceiving adverse cumulative impacts from numerous small sources.

CURRENT BUSINESS AND INDUSTRY EFFORTS

This section will briefly summarize the array of voluntary activities currently being taken by business and industry to prevent pollution. It is important to outline these activities in the NEJAC report on pollution prevention and environmental justice because it will help inform both community members and the broader business community about opportunities to improve environmental quality in environmental justice communities. Knowledge of existing success stories can inform future projects.

Regulatory opportunities for pollution prevention: The flexibility inherent in current regulatory programs has provided the opportunity to explore means to reduce pollution to a greater extent, and often more efficiently, than the usual command-and-control requirements prescribe.

Multi-Media Approach

Members of the business community have participated in EPA pilot programs designed to encourage pollution prevention activities. One such program, Project XL, promotes use of techniques to attain environmental results superior to those mandated by current regulations and policies at lower cost. The government offers the company flexibility in meeting existing legal requirements in exchange for enhanced environmental performance.[1] The program mandates community and other stakeholder involvement though various techniques which may include, among others, information dissemination, public meetings and hearings, community advisory groups, public comment periods, and consultation in conjunction with development of the final project agreement.

EPA and industry have implemented Project XL programs in a wide range of circumstances. For example, Merck & Co. reduced air emission levels in Elkton, Virginia by converting its coal-burning powerhouse to natural gas. Use of a cleaner burning fuel enhanced visibility and reduced acid deposition in the local community and a national park. In exchange, Merck received a site-wide emissions cap that allowed it to make changes at the facility without obtaining further regulatory approval as long as the cap was not exceeded.

Likewise, after holding eight stakeholder meetings, Georgia-Pacific Corporation instituted an equipment change under Project XL by replacing aging smelters at its

---

[1] The inefficiencies of regulating on a medium specific basis, especially utilizing command and control techniques, are well known. For example, a study by EPA and Amoco at a petroleum refinery in Yorktown, Virginia concluded that the existing cost to Amoco of $2400 per ton to reduce emissions could have been lowered to $500 per ton if Amoco had been afforded some flexibility. See National Academy of Public Administration, Setting Priorities, Getting Results: A New Direction for the Environmental Protection Agency (1995). See also, a criticism of EPA's command and control approaches in Jonathan Lash and David T. Buzzelli, Beyond Old-Style Regulation, J. Commerce & Commercial, Feb. 28, 1995.

containerboard mill at Big Island, Virginia with a black liquor gasification system. Gasification converts by-products from the wood pulping process into a clean burning hydrogen fuel. The technology will be the first full scale gasification system used in the pulp and paper industry. The new technology is designed to reduce air emissions by 90 percent, save energy and increase safety. In exchange, in the event the new technology does not function as anticipated, Georgia-Pacific will be allowed to operate its smelters without otherwise needed control modifications for a limited period of time to allow for installation of a conventional recovery boiler.

Other XL projects are identified on EPA's website, www.epa.gov/project xl. Although these projects have been largely successful in reducing pollution, the considerable transactional costs to both industry and EPA of utilizing pilot programs to craft special permits on a facility by facility basis weighs in favor of transferring the lessons learned from the pilot project to standardized regulatory programs wherever possible.[2] The need also exists to provide greater capacity to small businesses to enable them to identify, design and implement pollution prevention options.

Area Wide Approaches

Certain federal, state or local programs encourage planning to take place on an area-wide basis. Businesses have cooperated with governmental authorities in engaging in area wide planning, particularly in circumstances where multistakeholder cooperation can facilitate environmental improvement.

Protecting stream quality and flows requires participation of various water users and dischargers. For example, in stream segments where effluent limitations on point source dischargers are not stringent enough to implement water quality standards, the state must list those waters and establish a total maximum daily load. See 33 U.S.C. § 1313(d). The load is allocated among point source and non-point source dischargers. Businesses actively engage in negotiations to allocate the permissible load. Even absent the listing of waters as impaired, businesses may engage in multistakeholders efforts to protect resources within a watershed.

Similarly, under the Clean Air Act each State must adopt an implementation plan for the implementation, maintenance and enforcement of national ambient air quality standards in each air quality control region within the State. See 42 U.S.C. § 7410(a). This plan necessarily contains trade-offs among groups with an area.[3] Transit plans are frequently challenged as not in compliance with the state's SIP.

---

[2] The Common Sense Initiative (a performance -based system focused on industry sections), the Sustained Industry Project, and the Environmental Liability Program (testing the value of innovation in environmental management systems) are other examples of efforts to explore alternatives to command and control regulations.

[3] Businesses are active participants in the multistakeholder planning process.

ADVANCING ENVIRONMENTAL JUSTICE THROUGH POLLUTION PREVENTION
NEJAC Pollution Prevention Report
June 2003

EPA's Draft Title VI Guidance for EPA Assistance Recipients Administering Environmental Permitting Programs (Recipient Guidance) suggests that a government agency can identify geographic areas where adverse disparate impacts may exist and work with stakeholders to reduce these impacts, for example, by placing a ceiling on pollutant releases. Voluntary stakeholder techniques developed in the context of water and air planning may be translatable into methods to improve conditions within environmental justice communities.

Removal of Regulatory Impediments to Pollution Prevention: In some cases, current end-of-the-pipe regulatory requirements impede the kind of thinking that can reduce a much greater volume of pollution. The plight of dry cleaners provides an example of the challenges faced by small businesses both in implementing pollution prevention and in complying with the existing legal requirements. Dry cleaners use organic solvents that become spent over time. Proper disposals of these spent solvents, and control of air emissions during their use, are important concerns to the communities in which the cleaning facilities are located.

Many dry cleaners are unable or unwilling to invest in costly and time-consuming source reduction. In response, federal and state governments have developed programs designed to make source reduction more palpable for dry cleaners. While some of these programs offer only waste reduction advice to dry cleaners, others give financial assistance and grants.[4]

Recycling and Reuse: Use of recycled or reused products has enormous pollution prevention potential since such reuse not only reduces consumption of virgin raw materials, but it also can save energy and water consumption in the manufacturing process. Local and state governments, working with the private sector, have focused on means to increase the volume of recyclable and reusable materials collected, and to increase use of products made from such materials. Without product use, collection of recyclables is unsustainable. Innovations in collection include single-stream collection, which is more user friendly for householders and reduces vehicle traffic and thus

---

[4] One financial program is offered by the Pennsylvania Department of Environmental Protection (DEP). The Commonwealth makes "2% [interest] loans available to cleaners and others for pollution prevention equipment as well as the free site analysis program." DEP Programs, http://www.pdclean.org/DEP_Programs htm (Last visited August 9, 2002). The EPA has offered financial assistance to dry cleaners to achieve source reduction. This assistance included a grant of $100,000 to a Korean Youth and Community Center in California aimed at Korean dry cleaners. "This outreach and education program presents an innovative public-private partnership joining a private entrepreneur, a major university, and a community-based organization in a collaborative effort to advance to state-of-the-art environmental technology in the garment care industry." EJP2 Guide, http://www.epa.gov/oppt/ejp2/guide.pdf (Last visited August 9, 2002). Utilizing these programs achieves two ends: first, source reduction, which all stakeholders want to achieve and second, cost reduction, which the dry cleaners and business owners desire.

emissions in neighborhoods. Single-stream collection has been possible because of technology advances in optical sorting, a development pioneered by Recycle America.[5]

States and local governments also have begun to explore the potential to reduce the presence of particularly toxic chemicals in the environment through chemical- and product-specific recycling initiatives. For example, a voluntary mercury collection project initiated by the state of New Hampshire and Wheelabrator Technologies has resulted in the collection for recycling of 70 pounds of elemental mercury, resulting in a 37% reduction in mercury emissions.[6] Similarly, in Houston, Texas, the city initiated a residential electronics recycling pilot program to collect for recycling personal computers, cellular phones, televisions and other small consumer electronics.[7] Many communities sponsor household hazardous waste collection days that have facilitated the recycling of wastes that would otherwise have been disposed in municipal landfills.

Pollution Prevention Initiatives in Permits: The overarching obligation in environmental permits to assure protection of human health and the environment provides flexibility to employ creative pollution prevention approaches. For example, the City of New York, responding to community members' concerns about the number and potential impacts of waste transfer stations in several boroughs, used its discretion in issuing permits to site and continue to operate transfer stations to reduce the number of such facilities in communities of concern. When one company, Waste Management, sought permit renewal at one of its several transfer stations throughout the city, part of the permit approval included closure of other company-owned facilities, thus reducing the volume of waste handled and accompanying truck traffic in the borough. Such a policy, if implemented with regard to all parties competing to handle the same business, has the potential to improve environmental quality by consolidating activities at the facilities most appropriately sited and with the best environmental controls. Its goal is similar to the area-wide approach, but it could be implemented with an individual company or a municipality operating several permitted facilities.

States have piloted additional mechanisms to include pollution prevention in permitting. In California, Texas and Massachusetts, for example, technology certification is used to speed approval of new, pollution reducing technologies in permits.[8]

Environmental Management Systems: Many business, governmental and other organizations utilize environmental management systems as a voluntary means of identifying and surpassing applicable environmental requirements. An EMS is a management tool that ordinarily includes a policy statement, a process to identify

---

[5] See www.wm.com/recycle/ra_home.asp

[6] New Hampshire Department of Environmental Services, Environmental News (May/June 2001).

[7] City of Houston, Residential Electronic Scrap Recycling Pilot Program Begins (October 8, 2001), http://www.ci houston.tx.us/swd/press-electonicscrap htm.

[8] Kurt Strasser, "Cleaner Technology, Pollution Prevention and Environmental Regulation," Fordham Environmental Law Journal (Fall 1997), p. 28.

applicable requirements, measurable targets, monitoring, measurement and correction, and senior management review. Voluntary standards promulgated by the International Standards Organization and the European Union Eco-Management and Audit Scheme specify characteristics of the voluntary programs and stress the need for continual improvement.

By including environmental considerations in an organization's decision-making process, an EMS encourages decisions such as selection of raw materials, process design and choice of energy supplies to be made with an eye toward minimizing environmental impacts. EPA policies already provide some incentives for implementation of EMSs, for example by reducing enforcement penalties when violations are identified, promptly reported to EPA and promptly corrected.[9]

EPA should be encouraged to design incentives for companies to establish EMSs on a voluntary basis using techniques best adapted to the company's business sector and individual culture. EPA should also encourage legislation allowing multi-media, performance based approaches. An EMS can provide some assurance to the local community that voluntary compliance measures are accomplishing their objectives while simultaneously providing a mechanism to exceed requirements. In effect, an EMS is part of a method by which businesses self-regulate in alliance with the community. An EMS can readily incorporate measurement, reporting and improvement in areas identified by the community.

Emissions Reduction in Trading Programs: In order to implement continuous improvement in air quality while allowing economic development, the clean air program allows new development in areas not meeting air quality standards by conditioning the development on reductions in air pollution elsewhere. This trading program has enormous potential to allow development in relatively undeveloped areas while improving air quality in urban areas. In one example, the State of California approved a trading proposal whereby Pacific Gas and Electric obtained the emissions credits needed to construct a power plant by funding the conversion of 120 diesel garbage trucks to natural gas vehicles in El Cajon. As a result of this transaction, truck emissions in El Cajon were reduced by more than 50 %, with particulate emissions reduced by 80 % and nitrogen oxide emissions 50% below regulatory standards. Without the utility's purchase of emissions credits, the alternative fuel vehicles' added costs would have been prohibitive. That project was awarded a U.S. Department of Energy's Clean Cities

---

[9] See U.S. Environmental Protection Agency, Incentives for Self-Policing: Discovery, Disclosure, Correction and Prevention of Violations, Effective: May 11, 2000; U.S. Environmental Protection Agency, Environmental Auditing Policy Statement, July, 9, 1986. See also, U.S. Department of Justice, Factors in Decisions on Criminal Prosecution for Environmental Violations in the Context of Significant Voluntary Compliance or Disclosure Efforts by the Violator (July 1, 1991).

National Partner Award in 2001, which emphasizes the need to build coalitions and engage all interested stakeholders.[10]

<u>Pollution Prevention Components in Enforcement Actions:</u> Pollution prevention and enforcement are not incompatible. Where pollution prevention is undertaken as a mechanism to achieve or surpass compliance, room exists to enforce laws against non-compliant parties. Nevertheless, a wise enforcement policy encourages business organizations to develop systems, strategies and cultures that voluntarily promote compliance and improvement so that enforcement resources can be focused on the comparatively few companies for whom compliance education and incentives are inadequate. Pollution prevention can help ensure compliance, reduce the need for enforcement by promoting product and process innovation, use of management systems and community involvement, and allow enforcement resources to be directed in a manner ensuring full and fair application of the laws.

Pollution prevention interacts with enforcement in several ways. First, enforcement discretion should be exercised to allow companies exploring innovative alternatives to rigid technological requirements to experience a "soft landing". Second, consistent with EPA's current audit policy, the pollution prevention programs that companies are implementing should be considered when penalties are calculated consistent with EPA's current audit policy. Finally, companies can be encouraged to design and implement pollution prevention techniques in the context of resolving enforcement actions through supplemental environmental projects or other provisions in settlement agreements, decrees or orders.[11]

COMMUNICATIONS INITIATIVES TO PROVIDE INCENTIVES FOR POLLUTION PREVENTION

Corporate Environmental Reporting

Many corporations have developed voluntary, freestanding reports that describe a corporation's environmental, health and safety activities. In the past few years, corporations have expanded their reports to include social issues and the corporation's impact on the national and global economy. These reports are based on the reporting standard format of the Coalition for Environmentally Responsible Economics (CERES) (www.ceres.org). This organization attempts to enhance corporate responsibility, through shareholders, by requesting data on environmental topics termed the "CERES

---

[10] Waste Management, Environmental Review (September 2002), www.wm.com. See also U.S. Department of Energy, Alternative Fuel Truck Evaluation Project, Waste Management's LNG Truck Fleet Final Results (January 2001), www.ccities.doe.gov/success/waste_management.shtml

[11] U.S. EPA, Office of Criminal Enforcement, Forensics and Training, SEER Compliance-Focused Environmental Management System - Enforcement Agreement Guidance, August 1997 (Revised January, 2000). A SEP is an environmentally beneficial project that a party agrees to undertake as part of a settlement of an enforcement action and that the party was under no legal obligation to undertake.

Principles." CERES principles have since been expanded by the partnerships of the United Nations Environment Programme (UNEP) and the Global Reporting Initiative (GRI). These joint approaches help corporations set global standards on environmental reporting and the responsible use of resources. These groups have gained credibility among all stakeholders to the extent that many reports are deemed failures if they do not include the major components identified by UNEP and GRI. Another important component of corporate environmental reporting is the business-to-business information sharing activities. There are several trade associations that provide this service; however, groups such as the Global Environmental Management Initiative (GEMI) (www.gemi.org) do these activities exclusively for member-companies. GEMI is a leader in providing strategies for businesses to achieve environmental health and safety excellence, economic success, and corporate citizenship.

33/50 Program

EPA asked chemical companies to participate voluntarily in a national reporting effort intended to reduce the release and transfer of 17 toxic chemicals. Using the Toxic Release Inventory reporting system and baseline, the 33/50 programs sought to reduce by 1992 33% of the 17 chemicals, and reduce these chemicals by 50% by 1995. Indicating the effectiveness of voluntary efforts broadly publicized, industry surpassed its goal and reduced these chemicals by 55% by 1995. Moreover, reductions continued beyond the target program, with a 60% reduction by 1996.[12]

Information on Product Content

Consumer and public interest have led manufacturers to examine the content of their products. Many well meaning initiatives try to force, shame or regulate companies to make products containing either recycled content or use safer materials in their production process. The theory behind these initiatives is that fewer resources and safer material input will result in an environmentally friendly product. The reality is that market forces lead manufacturers to produce products that are not only environmentally friendly, but also satisfy consumer demands. Historically, command-and-control regulations have forced manufacturers to examine their operations and the effect that they have on the environment. Today, manufacturers are leading the way through innovation and research to produce safer products with minimal impact to the environment. For example, the Ford Motor Company has voluntarily reduced its toxic emissions by using water-based paint instead of solvent-based paint in vehicle assembly lines. Ford's switch preserves and improves the environment, saves energy and money and delivers a higher quality product.[13]

---

[12] www.epa.gov/tri/programs/other_federal.htm.
[13] See Ford Motor Company – Water Based Paints. www ford.com.

COLLABORATIVE ENGAGEMENT TO PREVENT POLLUTION

Brownfields Revitalization

Businesses and communities share a common interest in returning properties with actual or potential environmental contamination to productive use. The Comprehensive Environmental Response, Compensation and Liability Act, 42 U.S.C. § 9601 et seq., imposes liability on, among others, current owners and operators of facilities. The specter of liability inhibited prospective purchasers and resulted in abandonment of environmentally impaired properties. Many of these properties are in environmental justice communities.

In the past several years, states have responded to the need to rehabilitate such sites by establishing voluntary cleanup programs. The programs generally set risk-based cleanup goals that depend on the property's intended use, and afford protection from state liability when the cleanup goals have been attained. Requirements for public notice and comment often exist and community participation in reuse decisions is encouraged. Grants, loans and tax incentives are sometimes also provided. The federal Small Business Liability Relief and Brownfields Revitalization Act enacted in January 2002, provides incentives to redevelop Brownfield sites by conferring federal liability protection in various circumstances, including when state voluntary program requirements are met. The Act also authorizes EPA to offer grants to facilitate Brownfield cleanups. One of the criteria for ranking grant applications is whether the local community will be involved in the decision making process relating to cleanup and future use of the Brownfield site.

Encouraged by Brownfield legislation, businesses have revitalized impaired properties. Brownfield cleanups have ranged from small gasoline station sites to larger industrial facilities. For example, an abandoned railyard in Pittsburgh, Pennsylvania was remediated and converted to an office building complex under Pennsylvania's Land Recycling Program. Similar cleanups of industrial facilities for use as industrial, commercial or residential developments are increasingly common. Brownfields revitalization offers an opportunity for the business and residential communities to work together to their mutual benefit.

The focus in EPA's brownfields program on collaboration among regulators, community members and site owners and developers is particularly important when it comes to sites where the optimal reuse is recreational or "green space." Brownfields reuse projects that add to the municipal tax base can develop their own momentum, but non-economic reuse plans that function primarily as resources to community members need encouragement from regulatory agencies. The new brownfields legislation expressly includes green projects, and EPA has been active in facilitating recreational community enrichment projects. For example, EPA worked with community group members, local government, the school district and the site owner to transform the closed, remediated H.O.D. landfill and its buffer property into a multi-use recreational facility including walking and running trails, ball fields and a planned ecological education laboratory. To assure long-term environmental protection and provide "green energy," landfill gas collected at the closed facility will be collected and used to heat school buildings and homes. Similar brownfields reuse projects involving work group member Waste Management include development of equestrian trails, constructed wetlands, wildlife preserves, golf courses and a youth golf academy, and reef regeneration.[14]

Some of these projects have been certified by the Wildlife Habitat Council (WHC), which has developed standards for quality in development of new and restored wildlife habitats.[15]

Responsible Care

The American Chemistry Council's Responsible Care program obligates each member company to "achieve ongoing reductions in the amount of all contaminants and pollutants released to the air, water, and land." Each company practices responsible care by establishing a continuing dialogue at the face-to-face level with local citizens on any areas of their concern, as well as regular evaluation of the effectiveness of these communications. Moreover, each member company must establish an ongoing program to promote waste and release reduction by its customers and suppliers; assist in establishing regional air monitoring networks; participate in consensus approaches to evaluating environmental, health and safety impacts of releases; and assist local governments and others in waste reduction programs. The Council commits to continuous reduction of releases below health-based standards because "[t]he public does not endorse the concept of 'permitted' generation of wastes or releases to the environment. The public desires an increased margin of safety and environmental protection as a goal. If the [responsible care] policy is to address the concerns of the public, it must require sustained reductions."[16]

Dow Chemical Company's annual report on economic, environmental and social accountability illustrates the impact of the Responsible Care program. The company is on course to implement its practices globally by 1997. The company reports annually on its progress toward the goal of 50% reduction in chemical emissions, 90% reduction in process safety incidents, and 90% reduction in leads and spills from 1990 to 2005. In addition to employing the Responsible Care community advisory panels, Dow conducts community surveys to validate the effectiveness of these discussions. The company sets for itself the goal that surveys taken in the communities where Dow has a significant presence show at least 80% support by residents and leaders for the proposition that Dow is a good neighbor and a valuable member of the community.[17]

---

[14] Waste Management, WM Monday (July 22, 2002).
[15] See www.wildlifehc.org.
[16] www.americanchemistry.com/cmawebsite nsf
[17] See Dow Chemical Company, Public Report 1999 and Public Report Update 2000; www.dow.com/about/pbreports/00results/index htm.

VOLUNTARY EFFORTS

Product substitution/clean production

A principal method of reducing pollution involves designing products, selecting raw materials and choosing energy sources with the goal of minimizing waste production. Companies generally best understand their businesses and technologies, and can develop innovative responses to pollution if given the latitude to do so. When companies make innovative changes in products, processes or equipment, significant reductions in waste quantity can be achieved. For example, manufacturing changes in the chemical industry have achieved dramatic pollution reduction dividends.[18]

EPA required by 1999 that printing companies capture 92% of toluene emissions. Toluene is a chemical used in ink formulations during gravure printing. R.R. Donnelley in Chicago not only met the initial standard by 1990 (nine years before the regulatory target), but it continued on the path of continuous improvement beyond regulatory obligations. By the first quarter of 2002, R.R. Donnelley had achieved an overall 97% emissions reduction.

Sustainable production/renewable resources

Business commitment to production that minimizes impact to human health and the environment and utilizes renewable raw materials is growing. Often this commitment is embodied in a corporate sustainability vision. For example, General Motors has stated a commitment to integrating economic, environmental and social objectives into business planning and has adopted the CERES Principles. GM has stated its intent to achieve its vision through technology, innovation and partnerships with stakeholders including the community. As part of its focus on life cycle management, GM promotes recycling of vehicle materials. In addition, GM had reduced its non-recycled, non-product output by 42% by the end of 2000. Similarly, Georgia-Pacific demonstrated a commitment to sustainable forestry by implementing a program of third-party verification to ensure the health of the timberland managed by its suppliers. GP's audits include a focus on training, outreach, forestry best management practices, support for water quality, wildlife habitat and protected species, and guidelines related to daily operations.

---

[18] A study of waste reduction activity at twenty-nine chemical industry plants revealed that a high percentage of wastes could be eliminated through chemical substitutions and product reformulations and that lesser but nonetheless substantial percentage reduction could be achieved by process and equipment changes. See Mark H. Dorfman et al., Environmental Dividends: Cutting More Chemical Wastes (Inform, 1992) discussed in Kurt A. Strasser, Cleaner Technology, Pollution Prevention and Environmental Regulation, 9 Fordham Envtl. L.J. 1, 14.

Energy Efficiency

U.S. industry continues to become more energy efficient largely due to efforts toward sustainable development. U.S. industry's share of energy use has declined steadily since 1949, while its share of real Gross Domestic Product has stayed the same. (Energy Information Administration. Annual Energy Review.) Investments in new technologies are helping manufacturers realize performance benefits and greater efficiency. A few of these technologies include Combined Heat and Power Systems, which achieve high levels of thermal efficiency, energy efficient motors, and improvements in steam system performance. More effective use of energy by industry has the benefits of improving the environment through reduced emissions of carbon dioxide (CO_2), sulfur dioxide (SOx) and nitrogen dioxide (NOx), and creating a safer working atmosphere with better productivity. Greater energy efficiency has additional long-term benefits such as system reliability, and increased value to shareholders. (Alliance to Save Energy. Energy Efficient Technologies for Industry.) Voluntary efforts such as the Energy Star, AgStar and Natural Gas Star programs help corporations and consumers achieve greater efficiency and reduced emissions, while improving the bottom line.[19]

Conservation and Green Space Initiatives

An important element of pollution prevention is preservation of existing green spaces and creation of new areas that are not only non-polluting but also serve to remediate existing pollution. A number of non-profit/business coalitions have formed to sustain these preservation initiatives. The Nature Conservancy, for example, partners with businesses to reforest developed areas, preserves pristine habitats and restores coral reefs.[20] Many
102
States have dedicated funds to provide green space. The New York State Department of Environmental Justice Advisory Committee has recommended that these funds give due consideration for urban green space in order to respond to the needs of environmental justice communities.[21] Combining these green space-funding opportunities with community-based brownfields reuse projects provide substantial resources for community improvement.

---

[19] See EPA. "Methane and Sequestration" section.

[20] See www.nature.org

[21] Environmental Justice Advisory Group, Recommendations for the New York State Department of Environmental Conservation Environmental Justice Program (Jan. 2, 2002), p. 20. See also Environmental Law Institute, Smart Links: Turning Conservation Dollars into Smart Growth Opportunities (2002), p. 19 (www.eli.org publications), which indicates that among the many state smart growth and conservation funds, Illinois' Open Space Land Trust Program reduces its matching fund requirements for grants in "disadvantaged" areas.

97

Sector Identification of "Best Management Practices"

The Northeast Waste Management Officials Association, working with the lending industry, developed a pollution prevention guide for loan officials, educating them on how pollution prevention investments provide short and long-term returns. For example, the loan officer for Hubbardton Forge understood the potential liabilities extinguished by investing in a new electrostatic powder coating system and approved the loan. After two years, the payback was elimination of toxic emissions and 98% reduction in use of toxic chemicals.[22] The forestry industry through the American Forest and Paper Association implemented the Sustainable Forest Initiative, "a comprehensive system of principles, objectives and performance measures developed by professional foresters, conservationists and scientists to combine the perpetual growing and harvesting of trees with the long-term protection of wildlife, plants, soil and water quality." www.aboutsfi.org. Over one million acres are reforested each year under the SFI program.

RESOURCES, INCENTIVES AND CAPACITY BUILDING

This section describes current regulatory and financial incentives to encourage businesses to employ pollution prevention activities. Enhancement of these existing programs has great potential to expand pollution prevention in environmental justice communities.

Green Subsidies

Renewable Fuel Vehicles and Other Green Energy Incentives: Prices in the marketplace convey signals for conservation. They provide constant information feedback loops about the relative scarcities of different resources. The result of this information feedback system is that resource users have an incentive to "do more with less." It is these price signals that have prompted the creation of renewable fuel vehicles. For example, the Hybrid Electric Vehicle (HEV) is a general term for automobiles whose power train combines two sources of power: one electric and the other an internal combustion.[23] This technology can be found in the popular Toyota Prius. Another environmentally friendly fuel source gaining mass-production is the fuel cell, which is used as the primary power source in electric vehicles. Fuel cells work by chemically combining hydrogen and oxygen, a process that produces electricity and water.[24] Pilot programs using hydrogen fueling stations are already operational in Europe.[25] Another renewable fuel source is natural gas, which is stored beneath the earth's surface.[26] Other sources are ethanol and grain alcohol, which are made from corn, an abundant crop in the U.S.

---

[22] See www.epa.gov/p2/programs/primer.txt.
[23] See Office of Transportation Technologies, U.S. Department of Energy. www.ott.doe.gov/hev.
[24] See Fuel Cells 2000. www.fuelcells.org.
[25] See Could hydrogen be the fuel of the future? Marsha Walton.
[26] See Natural Gas Information and Educational Resources. www.naturalgas.org.

The new CLEAR Act includes important provisions supporting the development and use of alternative fuel trucks and needed fueling stations. Because these renewable fuels dramatically reduce the level of pollutants from trucks and other service vehicles, these tax incentives are vital to improving urban air quality in the considerable interim period until fuel cells are operational.[27]

Other legislative proposals support the development of projects collecting and transferring for beneficial use landfill gas otherwise controlled by flaring or emitted into the ambient air. Uncontrolled landfill gas has the potential to create a fire hazard, is odorous and contributes to local air pollution and increased ambient greenhouses gases. Incentives to go beyond regulatory gas control requirements and install gas-to-energy systems improve local air quality and provide clean-burning renewable fuel.

Brownfields Redevelopment Incentives: Federal and state remedial statutes require that contaminated properties be addressed to assure protection of health and the environment. To go beyond these statutory mandates and implement land reuse options that reduce current and future pollution often requires financial incentives. The Small Business Liability Relief and Brownfields Revitalization Act of 2001 have created a such an incentive. Total moneys available from EPA have expanded, and non-profit organizations as well as local government units are eligible for funding. The legislation confirms the importance of community dialogue about redevelopment options and assures that recreational and green space initiatives, as well as commercial and industrial options, will be considered. There are a number of other federal programs from which brownfields revitalization funding is available as well, ranging from the Department of Housing and Urban Development to the Department of the Interior.

State programs are equally important in providing incentives beneficial for reuse projects. For example, Illinois' Renewable Energy Resources Program funds brownfields projects employing renewable energy. The Wisconsin Department of Commerce awards brownfields grants to projects assuring a positive effect on the environment.[28] New York state remediation projects, which benefit the environment and have potential for public or recreational use of cleaned up property are eligible for grants.[29] Municipal governments also have taken the lead to inform property owners and community members about grants and other financial resources available to community groups and the public and private sector to move remediated sites into beneficial reuse.[30]

Subsidies for Installation of Green Technology: There are a myriad of mechanisms to incentivize and reward use of green technology, ranging from disbursement of funds

---

[27] See www.energy.gov/transportation/sub/altfuel.html
[28] See http://commerce.state.wi.us/CD/CD-bfi-grants.html
[29] See www.dec.state.ny.us/website/der/bfield/index.html
[30] See Cuyahoga County Planning Commission and Neighborhood Progress, Inc., Brownfields Information and Resource Guidebook (October 1998).

from taxes or special charges to issuance of bonds or outright grants. EPA advisors have comprehensively outlined these mechanisms.[31]

States also provide economic incentives for use of greener technology by, for example, requiring state departments to purchase at least 5 percent of all electricity from renewable sources.[32] In other states, business associations have advocated that impediments to installation of green technology be eliminated. Business representatives testifying before the National Environmental Policy Commission, convened at the request of the Congressional Black Caucus, recommended a number of mechanisms to fund clean business and technology, including repealing the tax on equipment installed to reduce pollution below regulatory levels and governmental purchasing preferences for companies employing green technology and pollution prevention.[33]

Green Procurement and Recycled Content Mandates and Subsidies

Green procurement and recycled content mandates have been found to be counter-productive, costly and burdensome to achieving environmentally friendly products and purchasing. Not all environmental gains have come through political action. Better progress has come from allowing marketplace competition and private stewardship. For example, Extended Product Responsibility (EPR) (The Road to Sustainable Development: A Snapshot of Activities in the United States, March 1997) stresses the idea of shared responsibility among suppliers, manufacturers, and consumers for reducing the environmental impacts of products throughout their lifecycles. EPR encompasses any or all steps in the process from the use and distribution of raw materials, to the design and manufacture of products, to the use and disposal of these products. The President's Council on Sustainable Development has stated that "The greatest responsibility for the EPR rests with those throughout the chain of commerce…that are in the best position to practice resource conservation and pollution prevention at lower cost." (President's Council on Sustainable Development: A New Consensus for Prosperity, Opportunity and a Healthy Environment, February 1996) Many companies have already taken the initiative by making recycling a high priority and integrating it as a routine business practice. Many companies, such as Alliance Energy, are using recycling in the construction of their facilities. Other organizations such as Enviroexchange, Wastechange, and Sonepa, connect producers of waste with those who use it in their manufacturing processes.

---

[31] See Environmental Financial Advisory Board, Paying for Sustainable Environmental Systems (April 1999), www.epa.gov/owmitnet/cwfinance/cwsrf/enhance/docfiles/other_doc.

[32] BNA, Daily Environment Report (April 24, 2002), p. A-9.

[33] See National Environmental Policy Commission, Report to the Congressional Black Caucus and Congressional Black Caucus Foundation Environmental Justice Braintrust (September 28, 2001), p. 100.

Research and Development Assistance

Federal agencies are uniquely positioned to conduct and disseminate the results of research on new and cost-effective pollution prevention technologies and techniques. The Department of Energy has been a leader in conducting and funding research into pollution prevention for radioactive, hazardous and solid wastes and generation and use of green energy.[34]

Grants from DOE can often make the difference in inaugurating private sector pollution prevention research, and the federal agency web pages are excellent mechanisms to publicize new technologies. Modest funding and technical expertise from the Department of Energy has been key to its research on the capabilities, cost and performance of alternative fuel fleets.[35] DOE's cooperative agreements to fund development of fuel cells, estimated at $80 million, are key to development of this low-polluting technology.[36]

Regulatory flexibility

Government regulations can promote or inhibit innovation and environmental improvement, depending on how they are designed and applied. Although traditional command and control requirements have reduced environmental impacts, they have also discouraged or prevented businesses from developing smarter, more economical solutions suitable to their own operations or responding promptly to changes in technology.

Various alternatives have been explored to introduce greater flexibility into the regulatory process and provide incentives for environmental improvement. For example, New Jersey's Gold Star and Silver Star initiatives afford companies with good environmental track records benefits to encourage further progress. These benefits include special recognition of the company, a single point of contact within the environmental agency, expedited permit processing, consolidated reporting, project flexibility, "smart permits" that authorize a range of operating scenarios contemplated by the company, and technical assistance with agency program requirements. Other available techniques for providing flexibility include innovation waivers of regulatory deadlines, special permits for testing and evaluation, and soft landing.[37] EPA programs such as project XL discussed above have provided similar flexibility, at times by allowing consolidated or multimedia permits. In many of these special projects industry has responded by adjusting processes or techniques to achieve pollution reduction.

---

[34] See www.em.doe.gov/wastemin; www.ornl.gov/ornlp2/p24 htm; www.pnl.gov/energyscience/06-01/inside.htm.
[35] www.ccities.doe.gov/success.shtml
[36] See www.ccities.doe.gov/whatsnew00.shtml. See also www.ccities.doe.gov/whatsnew01.shtml.
[37] See Strasser, supra at 60.

101

Single media bubble approach: When government has chosen to regulate by establishing caps on total emissions, allocating emission allowances to companies and allowing trading of those allowances, greater emission reductions have been achieved at lower cost compared with traditional command and control approaches. For example, the acid rain program under the Clean Air Act, which established a cap-and-trade program for sulfur dioxide, reduced annual sulfur dioxide emissions in the first phase by 50 percent below allowed levels. A cap and trade program for chlorofluorocarbons in accordance with the Montreal Protocol was also successful. The Administration has proposed a cap-and-trade alternative to new source review under the Clean Air Act and is considering a trading approach to discharges under the Clean Water Act. The success of market-based programs to date demonstrates that where businesses are given the flexibility to achieve environmental targets in a way best suited to them, both the business and the environment benefit.

The cap-and-trade approach holds particular promise for environmental justice communities. The government's usual practice is to provide less than a unit of emission credit for each unit that a company trades. The difference between units sold and units bought benefits the environment. Government could provide a greater credit for reductions achieved within an environmental justice community, thereby using the trading system to cause businesses to "trade pollution out" of environmental justice communities.

Regulatory Focus

The regulatory flexibility described above offers clear potential to focus pollution prevention efforts in environmental justice communities. Much like its approach to critical watersheds needing restoration, EPA could identify "priority pollution prevention communities" where the aggregation of polluting sources leads the agency to prioritize efforts to reduce overall pollution. This initiative should have particular focus on communities of color and low-income communities, reflecting the priority the current and past EPA administrations have placed on addressing environmental justice. Working with community representatives, the agency could identify its priority communities and focus available resources to incentivize pollution prevention. This could take the form of facilitating access to pollution prevention grants and subsidies, using regulatory flexibility to encourage pollution reduction, and encouraging comprehensive business and local government participation in pollution prevention initiatives.

Information

EPA already has established a network of information on pollution prevention projects, practices and opportunities that could be better communicated to both communities and businesses. The agency's web site compiles a list of pollution prevention projects and

ADVANCING ENVIRONMENTAL JUSTICE THROUGH POLLUTION PREVENTION
NEJAC Pollution Prevention Report
June 2003

resources.[38] Individual offices have their own programs.[39] The agency's "Partners for the Environment" program in the year 2000 included 11,294 partners who reduced 37.3MMTCE of green house gas emissions, recycled 17,788 tons of municipal solid waste, saved 768.8 trillion BTUs, and reduced nitrogen oxide by 158,172 tons and sulfur dioxide by 288,627 tons.[40]

The agency provides practical advice on how office workers and farmers can prevent pollution,[41] and provides extensive information on pollution prevention equipment, products and services.[42] All of this information could be made more user friendly by communications efforts that might include compilation of all information on an integrated web site, plain English description of pollution prevention resources and information for broad public dissemination, and staff training on the available information.

EPA can also provide important environmental protection by using its discretionary authority to issue "best practice" guidance. Previous work by the NEJAC Waste and Facility Siting Subcommittee provides examples of the ways agency guidance can shape local and state government and voluntary private approaches. These examples reflect ways that facilities with potential pollution can go beyond regulatory compliance to further reduce emissions and to assure robust community collaboration. For example, the NEJAC Subcommittee report on brownfields revitalization included recommendations about soliciting "green" redevelopment and conducting business/community collaborative dialogue that have shaped EPA and other governmental policies on brownfields redevelopment.[43]

Similarly, the Waste and Facility Siting Subcommittee's report recommending ways to reduce the environmental and health impacts of waste transfer stations[44] provided the basis for EPA guidance advising how state and local governments and public and private sector facility owners could go beyond current regulatory compliance to reduce pollution at waste transfer stations. These kinds of projects, combining the efforts of regulators, community-based experts and business, can generate best practice guidance that is practical, readily implemented, and directly beneficial to environmental justice communities.

---

[38] See www.epa.gov/opptintr/p2home/resources/epahy.htm

[39] See EPA, Pesticide Environmental Stewardship Program; www.epa.gov/oppbppd1/PESP

[40] www.epa.gov/partners/partnerships.html

[41] www.epa.gov/epahome/workplac.htm

[42] http://es.epa.gov/vendors

[43] NEJAC, Environmental Justice, Urban Revitalization and Brownfields: The Search for Authentic Signs of Hope" (EPA 500-R-96-002 Dec. 1996), www.epa.gov/compliance/resources/publications/ej/public_dialogue_brownfields_1296.pdf

[44] NEJAC, A Regulatory Strategy for Siting and Operating Waste Transfer Stations (EPA 500-R-00-001 March 2000), www.epa.gov/compliance/resources/publications/ej/waste/waste_trans_reg_strtgy.pdf

PUBLIC RECOGNITION

Government awards/communication of good practices

As evidenced in the number of corporate environmental reports listing awards received from EPA and state environmental agencies, issuance of public recognition is one of the simplest mechanisms by which pollution prevention efforts can be encouraged. Express recognition of pollution prevention initiatives that reduce and eliminate pollution in the "priority pollution prevention communities" described above would provide tangible reward for new business efforts to advance environmental justice.

Stakeholder Group Recognition

Many business and other associations designated sector-based awards for outstanding achievement in sustainable environmental practice. By incorporating links to these recognition systems in EPA's descriptions of its own award systems, the agency could acknowledge and enhance stakeholder efforts to prevent pollution.[45]

Multi-Stakeholder Group Recognition

EPA could facilitate a system whereby environmental justice group members could provide positive recognition for facilities and activities that have resulted in meaningful pollution prevention in their communities. In a time of limited governmental resources, creation of an award system recognizing activities praised by environmental justice and grassroots groups could be an effective means of encouraging businesses and publicly owned permitted facilities to strive for significant pollution prevention. Much like the Phoenix award for brownfields revitalization sponsored by the environmental departments from Pennsylvania and New Jersey, this award program could solicit applications from the public and private sector for sites or technological developments reducing pollution below environmental standards in environmental justice communities. Like the Phoenix awards, criteria could include the provision of environmental improvement and long-term community economic benefit, use of innovative techniques, and cooperative efforts by multiple parties.[46] The award's meaningfulness would be enhanced if its reviewers were primarily environmental justice and community group members. The awards would truly reflect community views and experience.

---

[45] See, e.g., the awards listed at www.americanchemistry.com
[46] See www.dep.state.pa.us/hosting/phoenixawards/Application/Intro.htm

FACILITATION OF COLLABORATIVE ENGAGEMENT

Interagency Working Group Template

The Interagency Working Group (IWG) was created by Executive Order 12898, "Federal Actions to Address Environmental Justice in Minority Populations and Low-Income Populations." Under Executive Order 12898, federal agencies are directed to make achieving environmental justice an integral part of their missions. The IWG is a collaborative demonstration project-based approach, with the federal government as the facilitator that allows for the full exhaustion and dissemination of information by all stakeholders. It tackles a manageable set of issues and parties, and allows for trial and error. Where good models emerge from the demonstration projects, they can be replicated and expanded in future efforts. Bad ideas can be discarded. Business is approached as a potential partner, is part of the dialogue, and is expected to contribute fairly based on its contribution to the problem presented.

Expansion of IWG Pilots with Funded Pollution Prevention Projects: The EPA is conducting the next round of demonstration projects, which will build upon the creative and comprehensive solutions that the last projects accomplished. These projects could be a good opportunity to encourage pollution prevention projects in environmental justice communities. To accomplish this, however, funds should be allocated, through EPA to businesses for research and innovative solutions to pollution prevention.

Supplemental Environmental Projects (SEPs)

EPA will frequently allow a company alleged to have violated an environmental law to perform a supplemental environmental project ("SEP") as part of an enforcement settlement. To be accepted by EPA, the proposed SEP must be related to the alleged violation and go beyond actions that the company was legally obligated to undertake. While SEPs may benefit the entity in violation, SEPs do not completely offset monetary penalties, nor will EPA, typically, accept a dollar for dollar reduction in penalty for agreement to undertake a SEP. With the exception of SEPs that implement pollution prevention projects of outstanding quality, which are eligible for dollar for dollar mitigation, a SEP will mitigate penalties by up to 80% of the cost of the SEP. In addition to the benefits available under the SEP Policy, EPA will reduce penalties further for entities voluntarily disclosing violations under the Audit Policy.

SEPs must meet certain requirements for EPA to enter into a settlement agreement that includes a SEP. By far the most limiting of these requirements is the need for "nexus" between the violation and the proposed project. The nexus requirement revolves around three axis: the type of media impacted; geographic area impacted; and nature of the violation. The further away a SEP is from these axis the more difficult it is to show a nexus.

ADVANCING ENVIRONMENTAL JUSTICE THROUGH POLLUTION PREVENTION
NEJAC Pollution Prevention Report
June 2003

Eight categories of projects are acceptable as SEPs. These include: Pollution Prevention, Pollution Reduction; Public Health; Environmental Restoration and Protection; Assessments and Audits; Environmental Compliance Promotion; Emergency Planning and Preparedness; and other. The SEP Policy strongly supports the implementation of SEPs resulting in pollution prevention, providing that "SEPs involving pollution prevention techniques are preferred over other types of reduction or control strategies...". [47] The SEP Policy provides for mitigation of penalties for Pollution Prevention SEPs. Pollution Prevention SEPs that implement source reductions are especially favored. Indeed, while as mentioned above mitigation percentages typically do not exceed 80 percent of the SEP cost, if "the SEP implements pollution prevention, the mitigation percentage of the SEP cost may be set as high as 100 percent if the defendant/respondent can demonstrate that the project is of outstanding quality." [48]

While the SEP Policy singles out Pollution Prevention SEPs for special treatment, other categories of SEPs related to pollution prevention are also included. An example of one of these categories is "Pollution Reduction" SEPs. Pollution Reduction SEPs address pollutant or waste streams already generated or released. These SEPs typically employ recycling, treatment, containment or disposal techniques. A pollution reduction project is one which results in a decrease in the amount and/or toxicity of any hazardous substance, pollutant or contaminant entering any waste stream or otherwise being released into the environment by an operating business or facility by a means which does not qualify as "pollution prevention." This may include the installation of more effective end-of-process control or treatment technology, or improved containment, or safer disposal of an existing pollutant source. Pollution reduction also includes "out-of-process recycling," wherein industrial waste collected after the manufacturing process and/or consumer waste materials are used as raw materials for production off-site.

To promote the use of SEPs that address environmental justice issues, the SEP Policy provides that EPA should consider mitigating penalties when the proposed SEP benefits a community with environmental justice issues. The SEP Policy provides:

> After the SEP cost has been calculated, EPA should determine what percent of that cost may be applied as mitigation against the amount EPA would settle for but for the SEP. The quality of the SEP should be examined as to whether and how effectively it achieves each of the following six factors listed below. . . .

> Environmental Justice. SEPs which perform well on this factor will mitigate damage or reduce risk to minority or low income populations which may have been disproportionately exposed to pollution or are at environmental risk. . . ."[49]

---

[47] See, www.epa.gov/compliance/civil/ programs/SEP/sepinfo html.

[48] See SEP Policy § E. Step 4.a.2 (May 1, 1998).

[49] See SEP Policy § E. Step 4.a (May 1, 1998).

SEPs must be undertaken by the entity entering into the agreement with EPA. While the entity may contract, or make other arrangements, with an outside party, the entity cannot discharge its SEP responsibility by, for example, agreeing to donate funds to a community-based organization or stating that a third party has assumed responsibility for the SEPs implementation. This is not to say that a community-based or other organization cannot have a role in either recommending a particular SEP or helping an entity to implement a SEP. Community-based organizations can participate in the development of a SEP by, for example, recommending to EPA that particular projects be undertaken as a SEP. This recommendation can be made either in advance of an enforcement action (e.g., community contributions to a Region's "SEP Library," a listings of proposed and model SEPs), or the advising organization can make a recommendation to EPA or the entity during the enforcement proceeding. Because the advising organization is not a party to the settlement and SEPs are entirely voluntary on the part of the entity, the advising organization does not have "veto power" or the authority to direct any action, in particular. Moreover, issues of confidentiality during the enforcement process (or other sensitivities) may limit the advising organization's role at the time of settlement.[50]

SEPs represent a concrete way for industry and EPA to translate the pollution prevention goal into action that benefits minority and/or low-income communities. While there has been no systematic review, case study examples show that Pollution Prevention SEPs have resulted in benefits to communities with environmental justice issues. As with other pollution prevention SEPs, these benefits can include, among others[51]:

(1) Environmental and health benefits directly attributable to the SEP;
(2) Indirect benefits from pollution prevention implementation "beyond" the SEP either through technology transfer within/outside of the firm, or through organizational changes within the firm. These benefits can yield both positive economic results for the effected entity and decreased pollution loading for the effected community; and
(3) An opportunity to turn a negative situation into a better or positive situation for all involved, including creating better relationships among the entity, EPA, and the impacted community.

The settlement of an enforcement action, or resolution following self-disclosure, creates a "window of opportunity," for the entity, EPA and the impacted community to address a variety of matters simultaneously. Especially for entities operating older facilities, in communities with environmental justice issues, pollution prevention SEPs can represent a significant opportunity. Benefits may include low opportunity-cost investment in

---

[50] See draft "EPA Guidance for Community Involvement in Supplemental Environmental Projects," 65 Fed. Reg. 40639-40644 (June 30, 2000).
[51] See OECA, "Final Report, Recent Experience In Encouraging the Use of Pollution Prevention in Enforcement Settlements" (May 1995)("Final Report")(Note language from this report has been incorporated without citation).

production processes, resulting in deceased operating and compliance costs, and increased effective life of the facility.

> [Pollution Prevention SEPs can incentivize firms, first,] to innovate, i.e., to overcome the barriers to pollution prevention innovation that often exist in firms, through penalty reduction, improved relations with the agency, and improved public relations... Second, since the firm has committed to implement the innovative project in its consent agreement with the agency..., there is a strong incentive to stick with the project event when technical difficulties arise.

For the surrounding community, these benefits may translate into reduced emissions loading, continued economic benefit from local industry, and positive business climate. And, for the EPA benefits include, efficient realization of its statutory mission. [52]

EPA should encourage collaboration between the company proposing a SEP and the affected community to design and implement SEPs that best meet the community's needs. EPA could designate within its Office of Enforcement and Compliance a knowledgeable technical assistance staff to facilitate the dialogue with the community, help identify potential pollution prevention projects and educate the company and community about the existence of proven, cost-effective technologies and innovation opportunities. Small and medium manufacturers with limited resources and expertise and the communities in which they are located would particularly benefit from this assistance. EPA should consider initiating these collaborative discussions proactively rather than waiting for a SEP proposal to be made.

BUSINESS RECOMMENDATIONS TO ENHANCE POLLUTION PREVENTION IN ENVIRONMENTAL JUSTICE COMMUNITIES

EPA reorganization

To enhance the prominence of its pollution prevention division, it should be combined with the Office of Policy, Economics and Innovation (OPEI), and regularized communications to promote pollution prevention activities in the various program offices should be assured. To better inform the public about EPA's pollution prevention activities, the agency should report yearly on FTE's working on pollution prevention projects in every agency office (including employees paid from the Superfund account).

Pollution prevention funding

EPA should request annual appropriations that re-establish its pollution prevention small grants. The agency should also make support for state pollution prevention programs a criterion for delegation of programs to the states.

---

[52] Id.

Enforcement policy

Where appropriate, compliance penalties in environmental justice communities should be directed to pollution prevention projects that benefit the health, environment and quality of life of community members, rather than directing these funds to the U.S. Treasury. Community members should oversee these projects jointly and facility employees in order to assure that community needs are met and improved collaboration between the penalized facility and its neighbors facilitated.

EPA information initiative

EPA needs to inform its staff and other stakeholders about the array of pollution prevention projects and ideas developed throughout its media-specific programs. To that end, its annual pollution prevention roundtable should receive the kind of financial support and publicity that its annual brownfields conference enjoys. During that conference, best practices should be publicized and rewarded.

Sector initiatives

EPA should approach the major sector trade associations to develop pollution prevention best practice guides and a list of contacts for further information. Pilot projects should be initiated with companies willing to try bold new approaches to pollution prevention. To encourage participation, the Agency should assure a "soft landing" in the event a new approach is unsuccessful, i.e., if new technology or practices not only fails to reduce pollution beyond applicable regulatory standards but is less effective that the standard requires, the company should be required to meet the regulatory standard by other means but shall not be penalized for the earlier failure.

State source reduction plan certification

State source reduction plans currently require a certification on progress made in reducing the volume and toxicity of wastes in the state. Facilities providing such certifications should be sent relevant, sector specific pollution prevention pamphlets and should be required to sign a certification that they have read and evaluated the opportunities described therein.

Small business pollution prevention coordination

Like community members, small businesses often have little familiarity with pollution prevention best practices and the regulatory and other experts who can facilitate pollution prevention planning. EPA should establish an SMM technical assistance department within the Office of Enforcement and Compliance Assurance specifically geared toward helping SMMs with compliance assistance and pollution prevention. This staff can work in conjunction with the advocacy and education efforts of the EPA Small Business Ombudsman.

Larger business initiatives

Larger businesses, usually members of national trade associations, are better informed than small businesses on pollution prevention opportunities, and the larger businesses

ADVANCING ENVIRONMENTAL JUSTICE THROUGH POLLUTION PREVENTION
NEJAC Pollution Prevention Report
June 2003

have the staff to underwrite participation in pollution prevention projects. Rather than the information and compliance assistance needed for small business, larger businesses need incentives for significant and creative pollution prevention projects. There are several means to incentivize pollution prevention projects in environmental justice communities:

- EPA should evaluate its XL and other pollution prevention projects to identify how to encourage the most cost-effective projects, including projects where technology or materials substitution could supplant more expensive end-of-pipe controls. It also should reconsider the level of pollution reduction expected in order to participate in such programs. If the bar is set too high, few companies will undertake the additional paperwork and process expected to participate in XL.

- Permits with pollution prevention projects could receive priority administrative processing so long as the community supports the projects.

- EPA could designate a single point of contact to assist in the processing of permits across media and authorize a range of operating scenarios in the permits.

- Special permits for testing and evaluation of innovative technologies could be issued.

- Pollution prevention projects could be favorable publicized by federal and state agencies, with appropriate awards and descriptions on agency web sites and pamphlets.

- EPA could organize an award system whereby a representative number of community group members from across the country would evaluate and recognize the best pollution prevention projects in environmental justice communities.

Recycling
EPA should investigate how its purchasing and permitting authorities could be used to further support the market for products made from recycled materials.

Household hazardous waste
EPA should further support creation of household hazardous waste programs, including disseminating information about the need for such programs. The EPA Small Business Ombudsman should promote the proper storage and disposal of small quantity generator hazardous waste to SMMs.

Performance and market based approaches
EPA should avoid rigid command and control regulations and instead employ performance-based requirements and market based approaches that provide incentives and flexibility to businesses to meet environmental standards.

CHAPTER 6: GOVERNMENT PERSPECTIVES

This chapter was authored by members of the Government Stakeholder group to elaborate on the views of the members of that group, not necessarily reflect the views of members of other stakeholder groups or of the NEJAC Executive Council.

HISTORICAL AND REGULATORY FOOTPRINTS

With the publication of Rachel Carson's book *Silent Spring* in 1962, the modern environmental movement quietly began. The environmental movement had transformed from the conservationism era to a new form of environmentalism that now considered the impacts on human populations as well as the natural environment. Carson's book, one of many important antecedents to the new environmentalism, detailed a potential correlation between the overuse of pesticide and diminishing songbird populations. Many readers became understandably concerned over this perceived environmental threat. However, many more feared the parallel implications that environmental exploitation could possibly have on human populations. The correlation of environmental misuse and its effect on living species reinforced the concept that we should appropriately manage our environment to minimize the effects of pollutants on our resources.

Over the years our population grew and industrialization expanded. The steadily increasing concern about the air and water quality resulted in significant government intervention in 1970 when the National Environmental Policy Act was adopted on New Year's Day. The tasks detailed within this new law would measure, assess, and evaluate the status of air and water quality existing at that time. Later that year, on April 22, the first Earth Day was celebrated. The final, and perhaps most significant, actions that occurred in the "Year of the Environment" were the formation of an independent government agency tasked with the management of our environment, the United States Environmental Protection Agency (USEPA), and the adoption of the Clean Air Act of 1970 (CAA).

Adoption of the CAA instituted the control activities of the newly formed EPA and began a history of regulatory limitation, or permitting programs, designed to regulate the amount(s) of pollution businesses, companies, government agencies and industries could release to the environment. This system proved immediately successful in reducing environmental impacts. Other regulatory adoptions soon followed:[53] These include the Federal Environmental Pesticide Control Act of 1972; the Water Pollution Control Act amendments of 1972; the Ocean Dumping Act of 1972; the Safe Drinking Water Act of 1974; the Toxic Substances Control Act of 1976; the Resource Recovery and Conservation Act of 1976; and, the Clean Water Act in 1977.

---

[53] See: Phipps, Erica, Pollution Prevention Concepts and Principles. University of Michigan, National Pollution Prevention Center for Higher Education. September 1995.

Further regulations were adopted to address the growing concerns over past actions of environmental polluters. These regulations would prioritize and tackle the cleanup or remediation of areas previously contaminated by spills, releases or dumping activities. Of particular importance was the authorization of the Comprehensive Environmental Response Compensation and Liability Act (CERCLA) in 1980 with the formation of a Superfund to finance the potentially huge environmental clean-up costs.

Many of the adopted control programs were very successful. Other programs were modified and improved, or perhaps eliminated because of a duplication of efforts. Numerous federal programs were delegated to the states and managed under appointed authority accordingly. However, as time passed, it became obvious that the regulatory control activities could be fully supported, or even expanded, to include activities that address pollution before its release into the environment. This realization led to the formation and adoption of the Pollution Prevention Act (PPA) of 1990. Tragic chemical release occurring such as Bhopal, India in 1984, where 2500 deaths occurred and in the town of Institute, Virginia in 1985, where no fatalities occurred contributed to this realization. This policy directed that pollution should be prevented or reduced at the source whenever feasible. It also expanded the base of the individual's right to know of the risks posed to the community. Instead of reiterating the "end of pipe" treatment of environmental pollutants, "pollution prevention" moved upstream to prevent the pollutants from being generated in the first place. Government at all levels has been encouraged to implement the conditions contained in the PPA of 1990. This realization coupled with decades of great concerns related to minorities and low income populations bearing disproportionate health and environmental effects led to the issuance of the executive order. This executive order encouraged federal agencies to address the issue of environmental justice.

This expanded reporting of emissions also proved beneficial to industry. For the first time many facilities actually quantified the pollutants released (and material wasted), and based on this information improved efficiencies and focused resources. Additionally, the public availability of this information can enhance both corporate image and profitability.

POLLUTION PREVENTION AND ENVIRONMENTAL JUSTICE

Pollution prevention (P2) is the reduction or elimination of wastes and pollutants at the source. By reducing the use and production of hazardous substances, and by operating more efficiently we protect human health, strengthen our economic well being, and preserve the environment. Pollution prevention encompasses a wide variety of activities including:

- More efficient use of materials, water energy and other resources
- Substituting less harmful substances for hazardous ones
- Eliminating toxic substances from the production process
- Developing new uses for existing chemicals and processes

112

- Recycling and reuse
- Conserving natural resources

Reducing pollution at its source (source reduction) allows for the greatest and quickest improvements in environmental protection by avoiding the generation of waste and harmful emissions. Source reduction helps to make the regulatory system more efficient by reducing the need for end-of-pipe [after generation] environmental control by government.

The process of pollution prevention involves identification, resolution, and action. First, government, business, consumers — society, in general — must identify the root causes of waste and pollutants. After identifying the sources, a decision must be made as to how best to minimize the generation of these wastes and pollutants. Assessing the efficiency, appropriateness, and feasibility of the method(s) to be applied can do this. Finally, action must be taken, resolving to implement the plan that best reduces the production of wastes and pollutants. Throughout this three-step process, the government can act definitively and reliably as an enabling partner in fostering pollution prevention.

Additionally, pollution prevention involves multi-media approaches that work to solve environmental problems holistically and do not only focus on pollution in a single medium (air, land, or water). Rules, regulations, and solutions that are not multi-media sometimes make existing problems worse. Such approaches can result in the transfer of pollution from one medium to another. For example, in some cases, by requiring hazardous air emission controls for industrial facilities, other problems might result, such as pollutants being transferred to underground drinking water.

QUESTIONS AND RESOLUTIONS CONCERNING POLLUTION PREVENTION AND ENVIRONMENTAL JUSTICE

The thread throughout the Principles of Environmental Justice, drafted at the First National People of Color Environmental Leadership Summit in 1991, is a call for pollution prevention. The Principles demand the "cessation of the production of all toxins, hazardous wastes, and radioactive materials …" (Principle 6.) They underscore a right to "ethical, balanced and responsible uses of land and renewable resources in the interest of a sustainable planet …" (Principle 4.) Nevertheless, without clear statutory mandates or funding imperatives, both Pollution Prevention (P2) and Environmental Justice (EJ) has been embraced slowly as core initiatives within government. Typically, environmental justice and pollution prevention are among the first programs to lose funding in a budget crisis. Both programs often garner marginal status in comparison to programs with regulatory foundation, such as air, drinking water, and solid waste. As a result, a marriage between the two programs is at times tenuous and even unattainable, but nonetheless important. Attainment could otherwise be realized by attaching the principles of environmental justice and pollution prevention to programs with statutory mandates and/or funding. Furthermore, the slow embrace has started to quicken:

Government and other stakeholders are implementing several key initiatives that are aimed at supporting pollution prevention and environmental justice.

Yet another question arises when we consider how environmental justice programs and pollution prevention programs are implemented. Environmental justice programs often call for additional scrutiny where environmental-decision-making, permitting decisions, environmental impact reports or other environmental review mechanisms relate to disenfranchised communities. Most pollution prevention programs focus on broad public benefits without respect to any particular community, race, or income. The goal of pollution prevention is to prevent pollution for everyone, not a particular sector. Yet, it can be argued that communities of color, low-income and disenfranchised communities host facilities using the oldest technologies. Where these communities also carry a disproportionate share of industrial facilities there should be a natural draw for pollution prevention initiatives.

It is obvious that both environmental justice and pollution prevention appear to have similar goals; however, their implementation can sometimes have divergent effects. For example, pollution prevention strategies may be costly to small industries in communities with perceived environmental justice concerns. The cost could force some business to think about closure. Nevertheless, the benefits that can be derived from these pollution prevention strategies far outweigh the perceived negative effects.

For instance, pollution prevention programs have resulted in improved health, social and economic conditions, along with aesthetic improvements in the community. Currently, some states are moving to support small business pollution prevention activities through innovative projects such as Environmental Results Program (ERP) in Maryland. In this context, the Maryland Department of Environment (MDE) encourages pollution prevention as a tool to achieve compliance. This approach has proven to be very popular among business interest and community members in the piloted Maryland community. The use of pollution prevention as a tool to compliance and to promote environmental justice is an example of how local, federal, and state governments, and industry, and organizations can collaborate their efforts to attain desirable outcomes for all stakeholders.

Additionally, pollution prevention, like environmental justice, is often difficult to measure in terms those regulatory agencies and legislatures use to interpret the success or efficacy of programs. Enforcement programs can tally dollars collected or actions filed. Media-specific programs such as air, water, or waste can point to actual pounds of pollution emitted or discharged, thereby gauging pounds of pollution reduced or eliminated. It is difficult, on the other hand, to calculate totals for pollution *prevented* from entering the environment. In essence, this pollution never existed and therefore cannot be measured. Similarly, it would be difficult to assign a numerical figure to the number of facilities that are *not* sited in communities of color or low-income

ADVANCING ENVIRONMENTAL JUSTICE THROUGH POLLUTION PREVENTION
NEJAC Pollution Prevention Report
June 2003

communities. To fully quantify the positive impacts of pollution prevention and environmental justice may require a significant shift in environmental regulation.

One approach for elevating environmental justice and pollution prevention on the EPA's priority list may be to engage the Environmental Council of States (ECOS). ECOS is the national non-profit, non-partisan association of state and territorial environmental commissioners. ECOS touts the membership of the environmental commissioners of 51 of the 55 U.S. states and territories. Its mission is to champion the role of states in environmental management through, among other methods, promoting state positions on environmental issues to Congress, federal agencies, and the public. ECOS works with EPA through EPA's Assistant Administrator for Congressional and Intergovernmental Relations.

GOVERNMENTAL INTEGRATION OF POLLUTION PREVENTION AND ENVIRONMENTAL JUSTICE

The United States Environmental Protection Agency (USEPA) has tried to encourage the use of pollution prevention within environmental justice communities. Pollution prevention was promoted as another available tool for use as these communities addressed environmental concerns. The EJP2 Grant Program was established to promote pollution prevention in environmental justice communities. EJP2 provided funding to qualified applicants for pollution prevention projects in environmental justice communities. Any non-profit, local, or tribal organization could submit an application for funding. Applicants were required to demonstrate that they worked with affected communities on pollution prevention initiatives and that they could garner substantial community involvement. Organizations could also foster partnerships between local industries and the environmental justice community. The EJP2 Grant Program was a starting point for pollution prevention in several minority and low-income communities. The program funding was eliminated in FY 2002. It is uncertain whether the program will regain funding in the future.

This disproportionate exposure to environmental hazards in environmental justice communities may be a result not only of industrial discharges but also of occupational exposure.[54] Pollution prevention is an effective tool in addressing both sources of exposure. Sometimes a facility may claim that implementing pollution prevention strategies may be costly and use this as an excuse for draconian actions (such as shutting down). However, this may really result from the confusion between pollution *prevention* and pollution *control*. This confusion can result in apparent tension between environmental justice and pollution prevention. *(note – good point but should be moved for the flow)*

---

[54] Geiser, Ken *Pollution Prevention and Environmental Justice: Some Cautions*, July 2002

Environmental justice and pollution prevention have complementary goals. However, the implementation of pollution control technologies can have unintended impacts on small business in environmental justice communities. For example, compliance with pollution control legislation may be so costly to small business in an environmental justice community that facilities choose to shut down. Thus, while the community may gain a reduction in pollution, which consequently may result in an improvement in environmental public health, they could also lose industry that may be vital for the survival (employment and diversity) of the community. Nevertheless, pollution *prevention* strategies, when implemented, can improve the efficiency and processes of these facilities resulting in increased profitability. A successful pollution prevention program can improve both environmental and economic performance. Pollution prevention programs have proven to be effective tools to reduce the costs of environmental management, occupational safety and health protection, environmental compliance, insurance liability, raw materials, and energy. This array of benefits cannot be achieved strictly by the use of control technologies.

The Pollution Prevention Act of 1990 (PPA) provides the federal statutory authority for pollution prevention. Several states have enacted state legislation that mandates pollution prevention planning and/or reductions in waste generation. Environmental justice has federal statutory authority and remains largely voluntary on the state and local level. Federal, state and local pollution prevention regulations act as regulatory tools to promote the implementation of pollution prevention strategies and programs.

FEDERAL GOVERNMENT AND POLLUTION PREVENTION

Section 6602 (b) of the Pollution Prevention Act of 1990 established a national policy that:

1. Pollution should be prevented or reduced at the source whenever feasible
2. Pollution that cannot be prevented should be recycled in an environmentally safe manner whenever feasible
3. Pollution that cannot be prevented or recycled should be treated in an environmentally safe manner whenever feasible
4. Disposal or other release into the environment should be employed only as a last resort and should be conducted in an environmentally safe manner

This hierarchy of environmental management begins with reducing pollution at its source. Source reduction perhaps allows for the greatest and quickest improvements in environmental protection since it seeks to avoid the generation of waste and harmful emissions. Additionally, the hierarchy includes recycling and other methods of dealing with waste after its generation. These four steps are all a part of sound environmental management — recognizing that source reduction is not always feasible. The Pollution Prevention Act requires industries to participate in pollution prevention. Section 13106 of the Pollution Prevention Act requires that every owner of a facility must annually file a

116

toxic release form for each toxic chemical released and to optionally include information on reduction and recycling activities for the reporting period. Furthermore, the PPA makes provisions for USEPA to provide matching funds for state and local pollution prevention programs through the Pollution Prevention Incentive for States (PPIS) grant program to promote pollution prevention techniques by businesses. These funds are also used to support state pollution prevention program activities that include outreaches to communities and local governments in addition to business and industry.

The four-step national policy for pollution prevention named in the Pollution Prevention Act does not stand alone in its efforts to prevent and control pollution. Congress has also passed several other pollution control regulations including:

- Emergency Planning and Community Right-to-Know Act (EPCRA)
- Toxic Substance Control Act (TSCA)
- Clean Air Act (CAA)
- Resource Conservation and Recovery Act (RCRA)
- Clean Water Act (CWA)
- Federal Insecticide, Fungicide, and Rodenticide Act (FIFRA)

Waste minimization has been a priority under the RCRA hazardous waste program for the EPA. Waste minimization is defined by the EPA as, "the reduction, to the extent feasible of hazardous waste that is generated or subsequently treated, sorted, or disposed."[55] The Resource Conservation and Recovery Act (RCRA) establishes the national policy on waste minimization. To facilitate RCRA implementation EPA classifies facilities that generate hazardous waste into three categories:

- Large Quantity Generators
- Small Quantity Generators
- Conditionally Exempt Small Quantity Generators

A business is considered a large quantity generator if it generates more than 1000 kilograms (2,200 pounds) of hazardous waste per month. By signing a hazardous waste manifest a facility certifies that they are taking steps to reduce the generation of hazardous waste where economically feasible and that they have a waste minimization program in place. EPA provides additional guidance to verify the existence of this plan for all three sizes of generators.

The Pollution Prevention Act was not just one more piece of legislation in the armament available to EPA. Section 13103(a) if the Act required EPA to establish a "[pollution prevention] office independent of the Agency's single-media program offices" and

---

[55] Mounteer, Thomas R., *The Inherent Worthiness of the Struggle: The Emergence of Mandatory Pollution Prevention Planning as an Environmental Regulatory Ethic.* Columbia Journal of Environmental Law. 1994.

§13103(b)(2) required EPA to develop and implement a strategy to promote source reduction. Specifically, the Administrator was required to:

> Ensure that the Agency considers the effect of its existing and proposed programs on source reduction efforts and shall review regulations of the Agency prior and subsequent to their proposal to determine their effects on source reduction . . .

The Clean Water Act of 1977 (CWA) is one of the many federal statutes that can be used to support prevention pollution. Specifically, CWA regulates the discharge of pollutants into U.S. waters, making it unlawful for any person to discharge a pollutant into any U.S. body of water without a permit. Under CWA, the EPA also has the authority to set wastewater standards for industry, thus controlling the concentrations of pollutants discharged. CWA touches on pollution prevention through management and oversight of what and how much of a pollutant goes into our water.

Similar to the Clean Water Act, the Clean Air Act of 1970 also provides opportunities to promote pollution prevention through air quality management. The EPA is given the authority under CAA to regulation the emission standards of several potentially hazardous pollutants (examples: lead, oxides of sulfur, oxides of nitrogen, ozone and carbon monoxide). Although the EPA must establish the national limits under the Clean Air Act for potentially hazardous pollutants, it is primarily the states' responsibility to enforce these limits. Some states enact laws with even stricter requirements for industry. The Clean Air Act, thusly, ensures that nationally there is a minimal standard that all U.S. industries meet. States with more stringent air pollution control statutes are free to implement their programs as long as they at least satisfy the minimal standards set under the Clean Air Act.

The Resource Conservation and Recovery Act, Clean Water Act, and Clean Air Act seem to provide the best opportunities to support pollution prevention. However, the Federal Insecticide, Fungicide, and Rodenticide Act (FIFRA) and Toxic Substances Control Act (TSCA) also provide opportunities to encourage industrial pollution prevention. TSCA governs the manufacture, processing, and release requirements for numerous chemicals that could have potentially hazardous effects on human health and the environment. FIFRA requires users of pesticides to take examinations to certify that they know how to use pesticides in a safe, responsible, and non-hazardous manner.

Regulated entities that fail to comply with these statutes may be subject to penalties due to civil and/or criminal enforcement actions. As part of an enforcement settlement, a violator may voluntarily agree to undertake a Supplemental Environmental Project (SEP). A SEP furthers the goal of protecting and enhancing the public health and the environment, and does not include the activities a violator must take to return to compliance with the law. Although the violator is not legally required to perform a SEP, his cash penalty may be lower if he chooses to perform an acceptable SEP. The SEP

118

must, "improve, protect, or reduce risks to public health or the environment."[56] The violator must actually implement and complete the SEP that is proposed as part of the settlement action. In general, the Environmental Protection Agency (EPA) requires that SEPs fall into of the following eight categories:

1. Public Health
2. Pollution Prevention
3. Pollution Reduction
4. Environmental Restoration and Protection
5. Emergency Planning and Preparedness
6. Assessments and Audits
7. Environmental Compliance Promotion
8. Other types of projects

A violator may also, as part of the SEP settlement, be encouraged to receive community input into the nature of the project. Violators who voluntarily choose to participate in a SEP must submit an itemized work plan for the implementation of the project. The itemized work plan might include: project concept, net weight of pollutant to be reduced, costs to implement plan, etc.

Federal statutes provide authority for pollution prevention activities. The statutes may be combined with SEPs to further promote pollution prevention. The regulations and SEPs are tools that can provide impetus to industry for responsible behavior that protects human health and the environment. These tools help set industry-wide standards, make permit limitations, and take enforcement actions.

The Pollution Prevention Incentive for States (PPIS)[57] grant program aids the establishment of state pollution prevention programs. This grant program has never been funded at the level ($8 Million) proposed in the statute. The funds available under this program must be equally (50%) matched by state funds or in-kind contributions. This match differs significantly from that provided to mandated regulatory programs that have to provide a 10% match. States may implement stricter industry standards (as appropriate to their local area) and make enforcement actions (because they can oversee their local industries more easily than the federal government). Since the establishment of PPIS, 49 states now have pollution prevention programs and 32 have enacted state pollution prevention legislation* with some requirements. Several other states have legislation with no explicit requirements.

The establishment of Pollution Prevention Incentive for States (PPIS) demonstrates the federal government's reliance upon the states to aid in pollution prevention. Many of the

---

[56] "Supplemental Enforcement Projects." U.S. Environmental Protection Agency. 5 Aug. 2002. <http://199.11.42.75/oeca/ore/med/sep.html>.

[57] EPA Pollution Prevention Incentives for States. Environmental Protection Agency. 19 July 2002. <http://www.epa.gov/p2/programs/ppis/ppispam.txt>.

national policies on pollution prevention, including RCRA, CWA, CAA, FIFRA, and TSCA leave to the states a lot of the implementation, enforcement, and opportunity to enact regulations that are more stringent. The next section, will detail the states role in pollution prevention.

SUMMARY OF STATE POLLUTION PREVENTION LEGISLATION*		
	Legislation	
State	Facility Planning Prevention	Other Pollution Requirements
Alaska		X
Arizona	X	
California	X	X
Connecticut	X	X
Delaware	X	X
Florida	X	X
Georgia	X	
Illinois	X	X
Indiana	X	X
Iowa	X	
Kentucky		X
Louisiana	X	
Maine	X	X
Massachusetts	X	X
Michigan		X
Minnesota	X	X
Mississippi	X	
Missouri		X
New Jersey	X	
New York	X	X
North Carolina	X	
Ohio	X	X
Oregon	X	

ADVANCING ENVIRONMENTAL JUSTICE THROUGH POLLUTION PREVENTION
NEJAC Pollution Prevention Report
June 2003

Pennsylvania	X	
Rhode Island		X
South Carolina		X
Tennessee	X	
Texas	X	
Vermont	X	
Virginia		X
Washington	X	X
Wisconsin		X

STATE GOVERNMENT AND POLLUTION PREVENTION

States have the opportunity to promote and encourage pollution prevention through regulatory programs (permitting, compliance inspections, and enforcement actions) as well as by acting as information clearinghouses–disseminating information about pollution prevention; and establishing and supporting state pollution prevention programs. Industries are required to meet federal, state, and local standards for pollution control. All state standards must meet at least the federal standard, hence, for the majority of industries compliance with state requirements means compliance with a more stringent standard than that set out by the federal government. In most states, pollution prevention remains a voluntary activity with no rules or regulations for enforcement.

The following are some examples of state pollution prevention legislation:[58]

State	Pollution Prevention Legislation	Goal	Operation
California	Hazardous Waste Source Reduction and Management Review Act of 1989	• Source reduction by large quantity generators • Reduction of hazardous wastes by 5% from 1993-2000	• Source reduction evaluation and plan • State provides technical assistance
Massachusetts	Toxics Use Reduction Act of 1989	• Waste reduction by regulation of toxic waste generation	• Establishment of Toxic Use Reduction Institute

---

[58] Yurcich, Stefanie. *National Pollution Prevention Roundtable*. 1997. http://www.p2.org/nppr_leg html.

State	Pollution Prevention Legislation	Goal	Operation
		• 1/2 reduction of toxic waste generation by 1997	for technical assistance to industries • Report Toxic Substance Report and Toxic Reduction Plan
New Jersey	Pollution Prevention Act (1991)	• To shift from industry pollution control to pollution prevention • Reduction of hazardous waste and discharge by 1/2 over 5 years.	• Requires reporting • State offers technical assistance • Funding provided by the Pollution Prevention Fund
Virginia	Pollution Prevention Act (1994)	• Voluntary pollution prevention through incentives and technical assistance for industry generators	• Information and technical assistance provided by the state • Incentive: waste generator reduction planners more easily comply with environ-mental laws.

Most states set their goals for pollution reduction and then set out a plan to achieve that goal. Some states require industries to report that they comply with the regulations, as well as reporting that they have a plan to reduce waste reduction. Many states have added technical assistance as one of the key components to helping industries reduce waste. This technical assistance is partially funded through PPIS and this service is often provided to industry at no additional cost.

Adopting pollution prevention practices and techniques often benefits industry by lowering a company's operational and environmental compliance costs. By preventing the generation of waste, pollution prevention can also reduce or eliminate long-term liabilities and clean-up costs. PPIS grants are usually awarded in support of the program areas of technical assistance, technical training, education and outreach, regulatory integration, demonstration projects, legislation and infrastructure, and awards and recognition.59 Three of the four states in the above chart provide technical assistance to businesses.

By preventing pollution, there is a greater likelihood that a company will comply with local, state, and federal compliance statutes. Virginia's program provides financial and regulatory incentive for businesses that implement pollution prevention strategies and practices that promote sound environmental management. Virginia uses this voluntary pollution prevention/incentive plan to encourage industry not to only comply with existing rules and regulations but often to go beyond compliance in pursuit of environmental excellence. An incentive program like Virginia's may provide a more proactive approach to pollution prevention.

LOCAL GOVERNMENT AND POLLUTION PREVENTION

The federal government recognizes that states are often in a better position to oversee their industries and can adopt more stringent pollution control legislation, as applicable and pertinent to their industries. Local governments are also a key element in pollution prevention and control as their scope is narrower than that of the states'.

Local government may provide resources for pollution prevention to both industry and the community. Some examples:

- Montgomery County in Maryland developed an EcoWise Program for Small Quantity Generators of Hazardous Waste (less than 100 kilograms –220 pounds – of hazardous waste in a calendar month). The program seeks to reduce the hazardous waste output of small quantity generators and address issues of waste management. Federal regulation allow for facilities that fall into this category to transport the hazardous waste to a permitted facility. EcoWise provides a monthly onsite hazardous waste collection.60
- King County, Washington established the EnviroStars program. The goal of the EnviroStars program is to give business incentive and recognition for reducing hazardous waste, while giving consumers an objective way to identify environmentally sound businesses. Envirostar uses a two to five star rating system. This program has received national recognition and has been adopted and modified by local governments in Washington and other states.

---

59 *EPA Pollution Prevention Incentives for States.* Environmental Protection Agency. 19 July 2002. <http://www.epa.gov/p2/programs/ppis/ppispam.txt>.
60 "Pollution Prevention Toolkit Brochure." Local Government Pollution Prevention Toolkit. May 1998.

- In Allegheny County, Pennsylvania, the local government has adopted and modified the EnviroStars Program. The program is recognizes industries that implement pollution prevention practices and strategies. The program acknowledges three levels of excellence in pollution prevention. To meet any of the three recognition levels, an industry must go beyond the minimum regulatory requirements.
- The Florida Hazardous Waste Management Program. This program provides pollution prevention training for local governmental agencies. The training assists in the development of a local pollution prevention program and provides necessary training for local industries.[61]
- California's Consortium of Pollution Prevention Committees has joined in on the pollution prevention effort. This organization is comprised of chairpersons of local voluntary pollution prevention groups. The committees organized the first National Pollution Prevention Week. During this week local government, environment, economic development programs, industry trade associations and environmental groups sponsor numerous events. The events focus on highlighting pollution prevention as a "way of doing business." Local government agencies "implement the activities such as pollution prevention workshops, 'model' facilities tours, storm drain stenciling, award programs, special training sessions, and resolutions and proclamations."[62]

In addition to training, recognition, and waste management, local governments also aid in the enforcement of local ordinances, promote recycling programs, and collaborate with communities in reducing pollution. Other local governmental agencies disseminate information to schools, newspapers, and households.

These examples demonstrate that local governments are an effective, and essential, partner in reducing pollution. Local governments can effectively collaborate with the state and federal agencies as well as local industries to support and promote pollution prevention.

TRIBAL GOVERNMENT AND POLLUTION PREVENTION

The concept of environmental justice can be difficult to apply to situations arising within Indian reservations. In most environmental justice cases, there are several kinds of entities involved, typically at least: a community comprised of minority and/or low-income people; a business that either wants to do or is doing something that causes environmental impacts that the community wants to prevent or stop; and a government agency that has permitting or other regulatory authority. Often there is more than one

---

[61] "Pollution Prevention." Florida Department of Environmental Protection. 19 July 2002. <http://www.dep.state fl.us/waste/categories/p2/pages/services htm>.
[62] "National P2 Week." California Department of Toxic Substance Control. 19 July 2002. <http://www.dtsc.ca.gov/PollutionPrevention/p2-background.html>

entity of one or another of these categories, for example, both a state and a federal agency, or more than one minority community that is up in arms.

In Indian country, the tribe might fit into all three of these categories. The people who comprise the tribe might be seen as an environmental justice community, in that they are generally considered an ethnic minority (and perhaps a racial minority) and most of the families may also be low-income. The tribe is, of course, also a sovereign government, and as such may exercise regulatory or permitting authority over the facility that would cause (or is causing) the environmental impacts that the community wants to stop. It is likely that, in addition to the tribe, a federal government agency or two also has some authority over the facility, but the tribe's status as a sovereign government is always an important factor in dealing with polluting facilities within reservation boundaries.

So, the tribe is the environmental justice community and the tribe is also a government with some measure of authority over the facility. In addition, the tribe may also be the business that operates, or seeks to operate, the polluting facility. The tribe might do this through a tribal enterprise or through a joint venture with a private business. Sometimes the tribe's role as owner/operator may be through a governmental institution, for example a utilities department that operates facilities such as wastewater treatment plants and landfills.

In non-Indian America, governments may also be involved on both sides of the regulatory regime, that is, as regulators and as operators of regulated facilities. There are usually some pretty well established walls, though, between government agency as regulator and government agency as proponent or operator or funder of regulated facilities. In Indian country, the distinctions between tribe as regulator and operator of regulated facility are often less clearly drawn and may be hard to maintain. Tribes, after all, are generally rather small communities, and community leaders often wear more than one hat. Moreover, people who perform roles in the tribe as government generally also perform important roles in the tribe as a community.

Pollution prevention offers many potential benefits in Indian country, in part because of the nature of the environmental protection regulatory system. The tribal right of self-government is particularly relevant in the realm of environmental law. Federal environmental statutes are administered primarily by states in cooperation with EPA, an approach that is often called "cooperative federalism." In the 1970's, when Congress enacted the first generation of federal environmental laws, little thought was given to how these laws would be carried out within Indian reservations. States were charged with leading roles, while tribes were left out of the process. In the mid-1980s, Congress began to rectify this oversight by enacting amendments to some of the major environmental laws authorizing tribes to develop environmental protection programs like those of the states.

Although the legal framework is largely in place for tribes to become partners in cooperative environmental federalism, and quite a few tribes have taken on some of the roles of states pursuant to the federal statutes, most tribes have not, for a variety of reasons. One important factor is that, unlike states, most tribes do not have revenue sources and tax bases comparable to those of the states. Another key factor that renders tribes different from states is the body of recent Supreme Court decisions regarding limits on tribal sovereignty, especially in the context of regulating the conduct of non-Indians. The Court's recent Indian law decisions have been criticized by many scholars for their departures from long-standing principles of federal Indian.[63] In response to the uncertainty brought about by the Court's recent case law, EPA has become increasingly reluctant to approve tribal applications to be treated like states for the administration of regulatory programs (except in the context of the Clean Air Act, which EPA has interpreted as a delegation of federal authority to tribes).

Because of such factors – having been invited into cooperative federalism fifteen or twenty years after the states, having inadequate resources to build programs that are comparable to those of the states, and the specter of having aspects of their sovereignty taken away by court decisions – the environmental regulatory infrastructure in much of Indian country is just not comparable to what it is in most of America. This relative lack of environmental protection infrastructure has been identified as a major environmental justice issue.[64] Pollution prevention can be part of the solution, by promoting economic development activities that do not cause much in the way of environmental degradation and, as such, do not either exploit the relative lack of regulatory programs or require the creation of regulatory programs as a pre-condition for development.

For a more detailed treatment on tribal governments, please refer to Chapter 4, *Tribal Perspectives.*

GOVERNMENTAL PARTNERSHIPS

The Environmental Council of the States (ECOS) exemplifies another governmental effort/partnership. ECOS was formed as a non-profit organization "to improve the environment of the United States." This goal would be accomplished through:

---

[63] *See generally* David H. Getches, *Conquering the Cultural Frontier: The New Subjectivism of the Supreme Court in Indian Law*, 84 CAL. L. REV. 1573 (1996); Phillip P. Frickey, *A Common Law for Our Age of Colonialism: The Judicial Divestiture of Indian Tribal Authority over Nomembers*, 109 YALE L. J. 1 (1999); Dean B. Suagee, *The Supreme Court's "Whack-a-Mole" Game Theory in Federal Indian Law, a Theory that Has No Place in the Realm of Environmental Law*, 7 GREAT PLAINS NAT. RESOURCES J. 90 (2002).

[64] Indigenous Peoples Caucus Statement, Second National People of Color Environmental Leadership Summit (Washington, D.C., Oct. 23-26, 2002); Dean B. Suagee, Dimensions of Environmental Justice in Indian Country and Native Alaska, a policy paper prepared for the Second National People of Color Environmental Leadership Summit (Washington, D.C., Oct. 23-26, 2002).

- Being a champion of the states' role in environmental management
- Providing for the exchange of ideas, views and experiences among states
- Fostering cooperation and coordination in environmental management
- Articulating state positions on environmental issues to Congress, federal agencies and the public

ECOS "conducts research on federal environmental programs that have been delegated to the states, state contributions to federal environmental databases, state environmental and natural resource funding, and state contribution to enforcement and compliance."[65] ECOS has catalogued the research and reporting done by the various states and facilitates the dialogue on environmental management between the states. As noted earlier the states are mainly responsible for support and encouragement of both pollution prevention and environmental justice. It is imperative that ECOS, as a facilitator of state dialog and cooperation, be a contributing partner in the promotion and integration of environmental justice and pollution prevention in state programs.

The National Environmental Performance Partnership System

The purpose of the National Environmental Performance Partnership System (NEPPS) is to improve and strengthen the State/Federal relationship and to improve environmental performance. Under NEPPS, the USEPA identifies environmental goals and then the states decide how those goals may best be attained. NEPPS establishes a partnership between the states and EPA and facilitates dialogue and planning. The majority of states participates in NEPPS with either Performance Partnership Grants (PPG) or Performance Partnership Agreements (PPA) and uses this as a platform to leverage resources and maximize possible environmental protection and results. NEPPS identified core performance measures for environmental results. The states have assessed under NEPPS that three pieces of information are necessary to measure the environmental results of a program. The three information pieces are:

1. Environmental indicators
2. Program outcomes
3. Program outputs[66]

Each of the three information pieces provides the states and EPA with different measurable outcomes. The compilation of the performance measures (collected throughout the 50 states) provides a national picture of environmental protection and will initiate insights on measures that can be taken in the future to improve environmental

---

[65] 5 Aug. 2002. <http://www.sso.org/ecos/GeneralInfo.htm.
[155]"Addendum to 1997 Joint Statement on Measuring Progress under NEPPS: Clarifying the use and Applicability of Core Performance Measures." ECOS. 5 Aug. 2002. <http://www.sso.org/ecos/projects/CPMs/JSA htm>.

programs. The integration of pollution prevention and environmental justice into NEPPS performance measures may be a desirable step in the future.

Compliance and Technical Assistance

Along with pollution prevention technical assistance programs, a number of states, and EPA, have implemented cooperative programs for compliance assistance. Cooperative programs work by aiding local communities, business, and industry in complying with the environmental regulations. Examples:

- In FY 2001 USEPA developed a Compliance Assistance Activity Plan inventory of 368 projects that focused on compliance assistance tools for new regulations and for existing regulations that presented compliance problems. The Plan also included activities that provide information to help the regulated community understand their regulatory obligations. USEPA developed compliance guides and other compliance assistance tools. These included technical guides, self-audit checklists and protocols, applicability flowcharts and expert systems. Additionally, the Plan provided overviews of laws/regulations, best management practices, guidance documents, and outreach opportunities such as training, seminars/workshops, mailings, hotlines, and new websites.[67]
- The Park Heights Auto Repair Project in Maryland seeks to assist auto body and mechanical repair facilities in complying with statewide legislation. Auto body shops are given an opportunity (voluntarily) to disclose to the state those regulations with which they are not compliant. The MDE then spends a year teaching the project participants about environmental regulations and what must be done to comply with the law. At the end of this technical assistance period, all shops must comply with the regulations.
- The Compliance Assistance and Waste Reduction Program for Metal Finishing Facilities in Oklahoma City. This program provided technical and compliance assistance to metal finishing job shops in Oklahoma City. Voluntarily participating facilities were inspected to determine areas of noncompliance and then assigned a "facility manager" who worked closely with the facility to provide education and assistance for waste reduction and compliance. There was no enforcement and participants were excluded from routine inspections while in the program. At the end, there was a full regulatory inspection to determine compliance with applicable rules and regulations and to provide a measure of success.

There are similar programs in every state. Some focus on industrial sectors and others on industrial processes. Some have a geographical focus. These programs provide

---

[67] Compliance Assistance Activity Plan Fiscal Year 2001, EPA 305-R-01-002 April 2001 http://www.epa.gov/Compliance/resources/publications/assistance/planning/activityplan.pdf

invaluable support to participating facilities helping them to improve processes and increase efficiency. When these programs concentrate on environmental justice communities, then there is the added bonus of community involvement and everyone wins.

Another cooperative grant assistance program is the National Industrial Competitiveness through Energy, Environment, and Economics (NICE[3]). NICE[3], sponsored by the U.S. Department of Energy (DOE), sponsors an innovative, cost-sharing program to promote energy efficiency, clean production, and economic competitiveness in industry. Through NICE[3] state and industry partnerships can receive financial support for demonstration projects for advances in energy efficiency and clean production technologies.[68]

The Environmental Leadership Programs (ELP) is a program that trains and supports (through grants and networks) emerging environmental professionals[69]. Selected applicants are provided with leadership training and they are then more able to share the knowledge gained with their communities.

Cooperative Programs can also be found on the local level. Local government and organizations collaborate with industry to provide assistance and education and reduce pollution. Some examples are:

- The Montgomery County, Maryland auto body initiative
- The Jefferson, King, Kitsap, Pierce, Snohomish, and Whatcom Counties EnviroStar Programs
- The Albuquerque, New Mexico Silver Management Program

These partnerships have developed compliance manuals, checklists, self-audit handbooks, best management practices, videos, CDs, etc.

Refer to Appendix III for additional information on governmental, voluntary and other partnership programs.

POLLUTION PREVENTION AND PERFORMANCE MEASUREMENT

Regulations, voluntary initiatives, and cooperatives provide the framework for pollution prevention. Applicants for funding of pollution prevention projects are required to comply with criteria that show partnership, a probability of success, measures of success, and collaboration with mandatory programs. Pollution prevention success and the success of pollution prevention programs may be measured in several ways. It is particularly important to use a consistent ways to measure the impacts of pollution prevention and compliance assistance efforts. These measurements can be used to:

---

[68] NICE[3], U.S. Department of Energy, Office of Industrial Technology, http://www.oit.doe.gov/nice3/
[69] Environmental Leadership Program. 19 July 2002. <http://www.elpnet.org>.

- Effectively communicate the activities and accomplishments of the state and local agencies to policy makers
- Improve program management
- Measure progress toward goals
- Provide those who fund programs with relevant activity and outcome information
- Influence policy development

One method for measuring success is mathematical. This means that the amount of a particular pollutant (pounds, gallons, grams, etc.) is measured at an initial point and then again at some future date. If the pollutant has decreased, then pollution prevention (or reduction) has been successful.

This method is used by many states to determine the success of pollution prevention because it is simple. This mathematical formula for measuring pollution reduction/prevention can provide a "snapshot" at a particular location but does not provide a national picture. Generally, these initial measurements are available when there is an enforceable regulatory requirement for industries to report. Many facilities are not regulated. Secondly, there is a gap in the data if regulated industries are not required to report the specific information. The National Environmental Performance Partnership System (NEPPS) has attempted to improve this scenario by creating core performance measures. However, there is still no conclusive national picture of accurate measures of pollution prevention success.

Pollution prevention reduces or eliminates pollution. Changes in behavior of government, industry, communities, and organizations are essential to attaining this goal. These behavioral changes are facilitated by an increase in knowledge about pollution and waste minimization, general environmental awareness, and public participation. The simple mathematical formula outlined above does not include these factors. Additionally, the method does not determine the reason for a decrease in pollution. For example, the reduction in pollution could be a result of lower production volume and not a systematic plan for reduction. The need to comply with environmental regulations is also one of the primary factors that can incentivize a company to invest time, effort, and resources in preventing pollution. Threats of fines, the danger of inviting additional paperwork, and concerns control and possible "jail time" contribute to this motivation. However, regulatory requirements provide influence only in cases where pollution is a regulatory issue. A different instrument may be necessary for measuring behavior, knowledge, and awareness.

A survey is one way to assess behavior, knowledge, or awareness. If the survey questions are properly framed the survey could gather valuable information to assess the attitude, behavior, and education of a community to pollution prevention. In environmental justice communities, a "quality of life" survey could be used. This "quality of life" survey could be used before and after implementation of pollution prevention legislation or voluntary initiatives, to determine and perceived changes in

130

ADVANCING ENVIRONMENTAL JUSTICE THROUGH POLLUTION PREVENTION
NEJAC Pollution Prevention Report
June 2003

"quality of life." A quality of life survey could address the aesthetics of the community, the status of health in the community, as well as the environmental education of community members. Maryland has proposed the use of quality of life survey as a tool for measuring the success of its ERP.

Education can also be measured by K-12 curricula to determine the extent of integration of environmental issues. A much more difficult measure is health of the community. Although a pollution prevention program may contribute to improving public health, assessing this impact requires careful planning and support of the public health agencies.

Hence, several methods can demonstrate that pollution prevention is a success. The method that most states have chosen is to look at net reduction of waste. However, looking at behavior, community involvement in environmental projects, and education can also measure success.

POLLUTION PREVENTION MODEL

For most governmental agencies pollution prevention is voluntary and the result of a very dynamic and fluid process. It requires flexibility, innovation, partnerships, and commitment. However, no pollution prevention project will ever make it beyond "being a good –even great–idea" unless the person who makes the decision about whether to implement a pollution prevention project is convinced of the need as well as the benefit of doing so. A viable pollution prevention program recognizes that decision makers in business and industry are influenced by both environmental and financial factors when they consider whether to implement a project.

Environmental factors
- Regulatory requirements
- The need to do the "right thing"

Financial factors
- The bottom line
- Gross revenue
- Quality/ Quality control
- Production
- Public relations
- Maintaining the "status quo"[70]

Environmental justice communities consider public relations as a top priority but it is only one of a list of factors that decision makers use. Sometimes these public relations considerations can be the biggest influence for government-operated facilities and

---

[70] Hillenbrand, Steve. "Selling P2", Pollution Prevention Review, Summer 2001

chemical manufacturers. In the case of small business, it may be a lesser consideration. This difference in priorities must be addressed when "selling pollution prevention."

An effective pollution prevention program must have:
1. The support of key decision makers
   a. Determine the appropriate motivator to use when promoting a pollution prevention project
   b. Identify those features of the project that appeal to this motivation
   c. Present the project to the decision maker with these features in mind
2. Defined scopes, objectives, and goals
   a. Set specific goals and priorities with all stakeholders
   b. Develop a clear understanding of the regulatory requirements
      i. What is required?
      ii. What requires "going beyond compliance?"
3. A means of evaluating options for technical and economic feasibility
4. Necessary and relevant training and education for all stakeholders with evaluation and feedback for continuous improvement
5. Funding
6. A method for tracking progress
   a. What is to be measured?
   b. What is an acceptable baseline?
   c. What is an acceptable timeline?
   d. Accountability/transparency
7. Recognition/Incentives
8. Documentation of the process and the results
9. The results can be used to help provide a more complete picture for the local population and to contribute to a statewide, and national, database of pollution prevention efforts and results. The compilation of results into national, statewide, and local databases can aid in the development of new legislation (if necessary) problem areas, or to differential oversight for some facilities, or the repeal of legislation where it is no longer necessary or effective.

CONCLUSION

There are some innovative pollution prevention activities underway at the EPA such as the Persistent, Bioaccumulative, and Toxics (PBT) Initiative, expansion of Right-to-Know requirements, and the promotion of environmental management systems (EMS). The federal government has played a major role as an enabling partner in pollution prevention. Regulations on the federal, state, local, and tribal levels help provide the framework through which industry, community, and government can work together to reduce and/or eliminate pollution. Through governmental partnerships, regulation, training, leadership, voluntary, and other programs, stakeholder groups can address:

- Goals for pollution prevention
- Industry and community concerns
- Effective pollution prevention strategies

Continued partnerships may be used to advance the complementary goals of pollution prevention and environmental justice. There are many opportunities within the existing regulatory framework for integration of pollution prevention and environmental justice ethic and rhetoric. Additionally, this integration may be applied to other partnership agreements such as NEPPS, PPIS, and other voluntary programs.

The role of ECOS should not be understated. The implementation of these voluntary initiatives happens on the state level. Without ECOS support the task of creating, and sustaining, effective pollution prevention and environmental justice programs are almost insurmountable. ECOS must demonstrate its commitment and support and must be an advocate on behalf of states for continued and sustained funding for these programs. ECOS could provide assistance to the states in formulating processes for incorporating environmental justice considerations into permitting and other environmental decision-making.

Currently all states have some type of pollution prevention program. The important issue is lack of funding and support for pollution prevention on both state and national levels. Although there are some federal funding mechanisms for pollution prevention and environmental justice the sums available are inadequate and continually in danger of elimination.

However, even with this limited support pollution prevention programs have used every creative means necessary to grow and direct many successful endeavors. Many of these activities, though not specifically aimed at an environmental justice community, nonetheless, have provided benefit to these communities. This benefit is a result of assistance and support to facilities located in and around these communities. This assistance helped these facilities improve both environmental and economic performance; helping to protect economic and public health. Admittedly, there is still much work left to do.

EPA must continue to set environmental outcome goals. EPA must then empower states, local and tribal governments to promote pollution prevention by allowing flexibility to achieve the goals using a variety of approaches— pollution prevention planning, technical assistance, multi-media permitting, command and control, etc. States' efforts can be evaluated by their achievement of the environmental outcome goals rather than the practice of mandated methods. The states must then be supported in:

- Developing mechanisms for integrating pollution prevention and community outreach on environmental justice issues at the earliest feasible stage. For

ADVANCING ENVIRONMENTAL JUSTICE THROUGH POLLUTION PREVENTION
NEJAC Pollution Prevention Report
June 2003

example, in the permit application process this would happen when permit applicants meet with agency staff at pre-application conferences.

- Use technical screening tools, Geographic Information Systems, Toxic Release Inventory data, and other information resources to help the regulated community identify potential environmental justice issues at the earliest feasible stage.

A pollution prevention program, whether federal, state, local, tribal, regional, or volunteer community organization based, can be effective as a collaborative effort to stop pollution. In order to do this, goals and objectives must be realistic and all stakeholders should be involved in developing the strategies to be used in accomplishing the goals. Pollution prevention provides a way of escaping the ever-increasing costs of pollution control. Effective pollution prevention programs are "win/win" situations. These programs help facilities reduce overall costs and provide economic benefit to the community.

Pollution prevention, once espoused as antithetical to environmental justice, is decidedly important for the attainment of sustainable and environmentally just communities. Unmistakably, environmental justice and pollution prevention advocates are recognizing the benefits of enacting these programs concomitantly for the revitalization of environmental justice communities. Government understands this and will continue to support, enable, and take its lead based on the currencies that emerge from communities, industries, and other stakeholders toward the betterment and revitalization of communities across the United States.

APPENDICES

**APPENDIX I: POLLUTION PREVENTION &
ENVIRONMENTAL JUSTICE CASE STUDIES**

**APPENDIX II: CURRENT POLLUTION PREVENTION
MANDATES IN   FEDERAL STATUTES**

**APPENDIX III: POLLUTION PREVENTION
PARTNERSHIP PROGRAMS**

**APPENDIX IV: POLLUTION PREVENTION WORK
GROUP MEMBERS**

APPENDIX I – POLLUTION PREVENTION AND ENVIRONMENTAL JUSTICE CASE STUDIES

Case Study #1: Houston Ship Channel Source Reduction Project

Presented by Neil Carmen of the Lone Star Sierra Club Chapter

Houston, located in Harris County, Texas is the third most industrially polluted urban area in the United States. According to the 1996 Toxic Release Inventory data, there were more than 5 million pounds of known and suspected carcinogens released in Harris County in just one year. In the year 2000, Harris County was responsible for releases of more than 23 million pounds of toxic chemicals into the environment and ranked number two in the country for the number of carcinogens released into the environment. The source reduction project took place in a community known as Channelview that is east of Houston and covers an area of over twenty miles. Harris County contains more than 1.9 million people and is 56% minority.

Harris County, Texas ranks number one in the number of oil refineries, chemical and petrochemical plants, hazardous waste incinerators and other industrial facilities. These facilities are responsible for the release of over 190 toxic release inventory chemicals and contribute significantly to the smog problem in the Houston area. In 1999 and 2000 Houston surpassed Los Angeles for having the highest number of one-hour high ozone day in the United States. On one of these high ozone days, girls on the high school track team and boys on the high school soccer team collapsed on the field. The area was also characterized by industrial accidents. In 1989 there was a serious accident at the Arco Plant, now known as Equistar, in which 18 men died. Again in the year 2000 two men died in industrial accidents.

The community residents who participated in the Source Reduction Project had lived on the fence-line of the facilities for more than a decade and invited Mr. Carmen to participate as a technical advisor. These community residents had previously been part of the community advisory panel to the Lyondell Chemical and Equistar Chemical Plants and had resigned and formed a separate health and emissions subcommittee to examine specific impacts of the plants' operation on public health. The companies did not agree that their emissions impacted on community health. So this was a source of disagreement and one of the main goals of the project was to create a two-way communication process that had not worked well in the past. The other key goal of the project was to stress pollution prevention instead of pollution control and that is why it was called the "source reduction" project.

ADVANCING ENVIRONMENTAL JUSTICE THROUGH POLLUTION PREVENTION
NEJAC Pollution Prevention Report
Appendices
June 2003

The project targeted specific chemical emissions of each plant that were selected for toxicity and volume and in the three years of its existence identified six citizen requests. The first was an aggressive fugitives emissions monitoring program. The plants had numerous leaks and fugitive emissions. The second request was to reduce flaring. These facilities had large flares that light up, create smoke and the emissions and odors from the flares crossed the fence line and were discernable in the community. The third request was an aggressive, reactive, predictive and preventative maintenance program. Here the aim was to address potential problems before they became accidents by installing triple redundant backup systems in the event of an electronic error. So this request focused on maintenance. The fourth citizen request was to reduce benzene emissions from a specific Lyondell process flare. The fifth goal was to reduce styrene emissions from a specific storage tank. The sixth goal was to reduce butadiene emissions from flare activity at Equistar.

Over the course of three years they were able to come up with a number of effective source reduction projects that were not very expensive and relatively easy for the company to implement. The community toured the facilities and the tours helped the community develop specific requests. The community also spent several months developing a matrix to determine which chemicals to target out of the 190 that were being emitted. The matrix was a chart to look at both the pounds of emissions versus the pounds of product that would be made from the particular unit and the specific chemical involved. The community group met on a monthly basis for four to six hours over a period of 3 to 4 years. The company provided inside information during the project that you would never find in the files of a regulatory agency. While the companies might discuss some of these things with regulators, the citizens got privy to information they would never come across otherwise. A facilitator, who was paid for by the companies, was very helpful. The planning and measured approach used in the project resulted in significant chemical emissions reductions.

Lyondell Chemical reported they were able to prevent over two million pounds a year of benzene from going to the flare by calculating a 98 percent destruction efficiency, that is over 41,000 pounds of benzene a year, that would not be emitted from the flare. At Equistar, in their East Plant flaring, they reduced chemical emissions from 261,000 pounds in 1996 to 74,000 in 1999. Equistar had previously been ranked number one in the United States in air releases of 1-3 butadiene, which is a probable carcinogen. Equistar had four different engineering teams that were looking at ways to reduce what they called "olefins flaring." Polyolefins are familiar to most of us as the little plastic baggies we get at the grocery store to put our veggies and fruits in. With the olefins, when they have a shutdown, they did not have a way to store or recycle the material. They had to burn it. So strategies were and are now being looked at to recycle or temporarily store the material.

137

However the request regarding the particular storage tank at Lyondell where the community wanted styrene emissions reductions was not granted because the company maintained that it would be too expensive to reduce emissions from that tank.

The project resulted in a variety of community benefits. These included reduced emissions and a potential for many more reductions, a significant reduction in flaring and improvement in maintenance and reliability. This resulted in benefits to the companies also because the companies always said that they wanted to do this in order to improve their profits by keeping the process units of their plants on line. The project also resulted in an increased knowledge of plant operations. This was one of the most significant things for the community people, because in these monthly meetings the company would come back with responses to questions and inquiries and this information exchange would never have taken place if there had been an adversarial relationship. The project did not involve any environmental regulators and the changes implemented did not require any permits or approvals. At the end of the process there was less hostility and a little less controversy.

There were benefits for the companies that participated as well. The companies saw reduced emissions, less waste, increased profits and a much a better image in the community. There was a focus on specific emissions sources. Plant personnel became more aware of community concerns about the specific chemical emissions. This was quite interesting, because, at the beginning, the dialogue between a lot of the plant engineers who weren't used to dealing with community and their interactions were rather chilly and difficult at times. However, as the project moved into its third year, these relationships improved even on the part of some of the plant engineers. Some of the plant personnel said that they liked the projects even though the projects are not going to make a lot of money for the companies, but they were relatively cheap and they were the kind of things that the companies can do to make the plants safer for themselves, their workers, as well as for the community. The matrix helped the companies understand why specific chemicals were targeted. As a result of the success of this project, other communities can use this process as a guide, and community residents can learn how corporations make decisions related to environmental issues and the economics and safety concerns those decisions involve. The project ended because right now Houston is under the pressure to reduce smog and cut their nitrogen oxides by 80 percent. As a result, the company representatives indicated that they did not have the resources to focus additional attention on the source reduction project and some hostile feelings reemerged. However, overall the project successfully reduced more than 2 million pounds of targeted emissions in permanent process changes and was responsive to five of the six community requests.

ADVANCING ENVIRONMENTAL JUSTICE THROUGH POLLUTION PREVENTION
NEJAC Pollution Prevention Report
Appendices
June 2003

Case Study #2: The Park Heights Auto Body/Auto Repair Shop Case Study

Presented by Bernard Penner, Tom Voltaggio and Henri Thompson

The Park Heights community in Maryland is a 96% African American community and the largest urban renewal district in the nation, but it is not a federally designated empowerment zone. It therefore does not receive the benefits associated with the economic and community development. This community was once an upper middle class community bursting with diversity and residential and business vitality. However, today the Park Heights community, like many inner city urban areas, has more than its share of crime, grime and abandoned houses, which have a devastating effect on family, children and businesses. The average income level of the residents residing in southern Park Heights is between $15,000 and $24,000. Almost 50 percent of the community receives public assistance. One third of the children live in poverty and in families headed by females. Over half of the units are rental properties with many substandard units contaminated with lead based paint. Approximately 35 percent of the youth are not in school. The teen pregnancy rate is about 14 percent, compared to the overall city rate of 10 percent. Park Heights has the fourth highest juvenile arrest rate in the city, with over 12 percent of these arrests among young people age five to six. The community has significant health problems, with over 3,000 residents that have been diagnosed HIV related illnesses. The community rates in the top five for lead poisoning, asthma and prostate cancer cases. Its residents, children and businesses have been neglected and overlooked when it comes to economical, social, environmental and physical development.

Park Heights is clearly an environmental justice community and this project, while still a work in progress, can be a model for improving the working relationships between the regulators, the regulated community and the residential community. There are three essential components to this project. The first component is dedicated to finding a way to talk about compliance rates that makes sense. This project aims to evaluate the effectiveness of compliance assistance to the auto body shop sector. The project goals also included improving community between the regulators and the regulated community, improving the quality of life in this community and raising the awareness of the community respecting shops that are doing a good job and shops that are not doing a good job.

There were numerous auto body shops located in a fairly small area and hardly any enforcement actions were taken in that area. Auto body shops were selected because the community believed there were an inordinate number of facilities and because auto body shops had multimedia impacts. There is an air impact, a waste impact and a water

139

impact. Regulators may not ordinarily think of the multimedia impact of a facility but people in the neighborhood have to live next to a facility. They experience the whole facility, and they haven't gotten the training or perspective on a facility to break it up into three different media. The project brought together and had the cooperation of three levels of government-- federal government, state government and local government-- because we wanted to get everybody working together to engage in collaborative problem solving. EPA headquarters provided $275,000 in funding, which aided in planning and design of the project.

The methodology developed was to delineate the neighborhood. Identifying facilities through existing permits and through existing regulatory structures did this. A representative community organization was also paid to go through the community with a global positioning sensor and match the definitions it saw because what the community identified had to match the project definitions for the regulatory authorities to have legal authority. One of the interesting things is that the community thought they really had a big, big problem here, and they did have a problem, but they thought it was bigger than it was. They thought there were 150 facilities in the area. It turns out we were only able to locate 50. Not that 50 doesn't present a problem, because it does, but it really does show the importance of grass roots investigation. An auto body facility deals in scrap tires, waste oil, volatile organic compounds and spray emissions from their spray booths. Each of those areas has a separate body of regulatory requirements. The project developed environmental business performance indicators in order to rank each area and the type of behavior associated with that area for each facility. The goal was not to automatically find a facility in noncompliance but to provide compliance assistance and identify behavior improvements as performance indicators.

For example, with waste oil, if the facility has a waste oil hauler that tends to indicate that at least they have an awareness of it. Maryland has a fairly intricate scrap tire program. If a facility has a scrap tire permit, that tells you at least they know they need to get a permit and somebody has looked at an application. If a facility has a spray booth, there is at least some degree of consciousness that they need to contain paint emissions.

They started with baseline inspections, from the baseline inspection we inferred where the problems were, and then began to render the compliance assistance. To assist in the baseline inspection, they created a baseline inspector checklist. The inspectors went down the line always asking the same questions. As a result of the baseline inspections, there emerged two different types of facilities. Some were familiar with the regulations applicable to their operations and others needed additional assistance. There were also two types of facilities. The project then developed a plain English guide for the auto body shops and a plain English guide for the mechanical repair shops. Using the plain English guide as a teaching tool and with the assistance of the community, the guide will

ADVANCING ENVIRONMENTAL JUSTICE THROUGH POLLUTION PREVENTION
NEJAC Pollution Prevention Report
Appendices
June 2003

be delivered to every shop identified in the community. Then again, using the guide, the project led training sessions.

After the training, there will be a period for the compliance assistance to be implemented and then there will be a final round of inspections. The inspectors, with their book and with their checklist, will go back and again inspect a random sample set of facilities. The goal is we take what was observed at the beginning of the process, observe conditions at the end of the compliance assistance process, compare the two, and try to understand what can be learned.

The anticipated benefits of the project are improved compliance, improvement in the quality of life for the people that are living in the community and getting the regulators, regulated and residential community all talking to one another. These workshops will create that environment for improved communication. The shops have got to be willing to participate, but if they do they are given limited amnesty. If they disclose a violation to the regulators, no enforcement action is taken against them. There is nothing unique in this. This is an environmental audit policy. The goal is also to improve the regulatory process. The regulators are able to gain additional information and the regulated community understands that it can come to the regulators for help in solving its problems.

Currently, more than 40 baseline inspections have been done and the plain English guidebook is in its final draft and is being selectively reviewed by several auto body shops to see if it makes sense. The training sessions are in the planning stages and the project is also planning the introductory training sessions to show the whole community how the project is working. But the compliance assistance phase has not been completed and there have not been any follow- up inspections. However, other communities in South Carolina and Florida have had success following similar models, so there is reason to believe that this project will also be successful.

141

ADVANCING ENVIRONMENTAL JUSTICE THROUGH POLLUTION PREVENTION
NEJAC Pollution Prevention Report
Appendices
June 2003

APPENDIX II – CURRENT POLLUTION PREVENTION MANDATES IN FEDERAL STATUTES

Federal Act	Section	• Pollution Prevention Mandate
Pollution Prevention Act (PPA)	13103	• EPA mandated to develop and implement a strategy to promote source reduction.
	13104	• EPA as administrator is given the authority to provide grants to the States to promote source reduction by businesses
	13105	• EPA mandated to establish a database that contains information on source reduction.
	13106	• Owners and operators of businesses that are required to file a toxic chemical release form must include a toxic reduction and recycling report
Clean Air Act (CAA)	7402	• Encourages cooperation amongst the federal departments, states, and local governments for prevention and control of air pollution.
	7403	• EPA mandated to establish a national research and development program for prevention and air pollution control. • Also, EPA must facilitate coordination amongst air pollution prevention and control agencies.
	7405	• EPA can make grants to air pollution prevention and control agencies.
	7412	• Facilities that reduce their emission of toxics into the air by 90-95% can qualify for permit waivers.
	7414 and 7418	• EPA may establish record keeping, inspections, and monitoring for all facilities that emit pollutants.
	Subchapter I, Part C Sec 7470-7479	• Prevention of significant deterioration of air quality-establishment of a plan that includes emissions limitations to protect public welfare and the environment.
	Subchapter II	• General emissions standards

142

Federal Act	Section	• Pollution Prevention Mandate
Emergency Planning and Community Right to Know Act (EPCRA)	11001-11005	• Emergency planning requirements for pollution and fire control. Provides substances and facilities covered under this act.
	11021-11022	• Facilities covered under EPCRA must have ready Material Safety Data Sheets for all chemicals (MSDS) and must complete hazardous chemical inventory forms.
	11023	• Owners and operators of facilities covered under EPCRA must complete a toxic chemical release form.
Resource Conservation and Recovery Act (RCRA)	6907	• EPA must establish waste management guidelines.
	6908a	• EPA may assist Indian tribes in waste management.
	6921-6925	• 6921: Hazardous Waste requirements established for owners and operators of facilities that produce hazardous wastes. Under 6922: Generators must certify in shipping manifests that they have a plan to reduce waste. They must also submit a biennial report indicating their efforts to reduce volume and toxicity of wastes. 6925: Permit required for treatment and storage of hazardous wastes.
	6927	• EPA can make facilities describe their waste reduction program and inspect them to determine whether a program is actually in place.
	6931	• Grants appropriated to the States for assistance in development of Hazardous Waste Programs.
	6981	• EPA shall render financial assistance to federal, state, and local agencies that are researching, investigating, or providing in areas of waste management and minimization.

Federal Act	Section	• Pollution Prevention Mandate
Clean Water Act (CWA)	1251	• National goal is to eliminate the discharge of pollutants into navigable waters.
	1252	• EPA mandated in cooperation with federal state, and local agencies and industries to develop programs for preventing, reducing, or eliminating the pollution of the navigable waters and ground waters and improving the sanitary condition of surface and underground waters.
	1256	• Appropriation of funds to state and local agencies for pollution control.
	1342	• EPA can put additional restrictions on permits (not included in the act).
	1381	• EPA given authority to make grants to states for pollution control revolving fund for implementation of management and conservation plans.
Federal Insecticide, Fungicide and Rodenticide Act (FIFRA)	136	• All pesticides and pesticide establishments must be registered. Non-registered pesticides may not be sold or distributed in the U.S.
National Environmental Policy Act (NEPA)	4331	• Congress recognizes "the profound impact of man's activity on the interrelations of all components of the natural environment."
	4363	• EPA shall establish a program for long -term research for all activities listed under NEPA.
	4363a	• EPA mandated to conduct demonstrations of energy-related pollution control technologies.
	4368a	• Utilization of talents of older Americans in projects of pollution prevention, abatement, and control through technical assistance to environmental agencies.
	4368b	• Provide technical assistance to Indian Tribes for environmental assistance on Indian lands.

ADVANCING ENVIRONMENTAL JUSTICE THROUGH POLLUTION PREVENTION
NEJAC Pollution Prevention Report
Appendices
June 2003

APPENDIX III – POLLUTION PREVENTION PARTNERSHIP PROGRAMS

INDUSTRY PARTNERSHIPS:

Government has collaborated with industry in a number of widely recognized programs. The partnership between federal, state, and local government and industries provides the opportunity for collaboration in developing solutions that address pollution prevention, control, and environmental regulations. The partnership facilitates pollution prevention by creating common ground for government and industry. The following are a few partnership programs.

Program	Goal	How it Works

145

Program	Goal	How it Works
Project XL[1]	• To obtain a partnership between state and local governments, businesses and federal facilities with the EPA in order to develop strategies for environmental protection	• 8 selection criteria including: o Production of better environmental results than those that can be achieved through regulations o Production of benefits (money savings, regulatory flexibility, incentives, etc.) o Support by stakeholders o Achieve pollution prevention o Transferable lessons o Demonstrate feasibility o Establish accountability (reporting, monitoring, evaluations) o Avoid shifting risk

---

[1] "Project XL: What is Project XL?" U.S. Environmental Protection Agency. 19 July 2002. <http://www.epa.gov/projectxl/file2.htm>.

Program	Goal		How it Works
Common Sense Initiative[2]	• Partnership with representatives from federal, state, local governments, community-based and national environmental groups, environmental justice groups, labor, and industry with the EPA to examine environmental requirements impacting the following industries.	○ Car manufacturing ○ Computers/Electro nics ○ Iron/Steel ○ Metal finishing ○ Petroleum refining ○ Printing	• Reduction of costs and burdens of compliance with air regulations in manufacturing sector. • Developing new ways to address iron/steel cleanup. • Making it easier for computers and electronics sector to achieve pollution prevention • Other projects relating to specified industries.
Performance Track[3]	• Public/private partnership • To recognize and encourage top environmental performers • To go beyond compliance with regulatory requirements • To attain levels of environmental performance that benefit people, communities, and the environment		• Facilities must have: • Adopted and implemented an environmental management system (EMS) • Commit to improving their environmental performance • Commit to public outreach and performance reporting • Have a record of sustained compliance with environmental requirements
Green Star[4]	• Encouragement of businesses to practice waste reduction through pollution prevention		• Education • Technical Assistance • Award Programs

---

[2] "EPA's Common Sense Initiative (CSI)." EnviroSense. 19 July 2002. <http://es.epa.gov/partners/csi/csi.html>.

[3] National Environmental Performance Track. August 14, 2002. http://www.epa.gov/performancetrack.

[4] Green Star. 19 July 2002. <http://www.greenstarinc.org/>.

147

Program	Goal	How it Works
Project XL[5]	• To obtain a partnership between stat e and local governments, businesses and federal facilities with the EPA in order to develop strategies for environmental protection	• 8 selection criteria including: o Production of better environmental results than those that can be achieved through regulations o Production of benefits (money savings, regulatory flexibility, incentives, etc.) o Support by stakeholders o Achieve pollution prevention o Transferable lessons o Demonstrate feasibility o Establish accountability (reporting, monitoring, evaluations) o Avoid shifting risk

[5] "Project XL: What is Project XL?" U.S. Environmental Protection Agency. 19 July 2002. <http://www.epa.gov/projectxl/file2.htm>.

Program	Goal		How it Works

Common Sense Initiative[6]	• Partnership with representatives from federal, state, local governments, community-based and national environmental groups, environmental justice groups, labor, and industry with the EPA to examine environmental requirements impacting the following industries.
	   ○ Car manufacturing
	   ○ Computers/Electronics
	   ○ Iron/Steel
	   ○ Metal finishing
	   ○ Petroleum refining
	   ○ Printing
			• Reduction of costs and burdens of compliance with air regulations in manufacturing sector.
			• Developing new ways to address iron/steel cleanup.
			• Making it easier for computers and electronics sector to achieve pollution prevention
			• Other projects relating to specified industries.

Performance Track[7]	• Public/private partnership • To recognize and encourage top environmental performers • To go beyond compliance with regulatory requirements • To attain levels of environmental performance that benefit people, communities, and the environment		• Facilities must have: • Adopted and implemented an environmental management system (EMS) • Commit to improving their environmental performance • Commit to public outreach and performance reporting • Have a record of sustained compliance with environmental requirements
Green Star[8]	• Encouragement of businesses to practice waste reduction through pollution prevention		• Education • Technical Assistance • Award Programs

[6] "EPA's Common Sense Initiative (CSI)." EnviroSense. 19 July 2002. <http://es.epa.gov/partners/csi/csi.html>.

[7] National Environmental Performance Track. August 14, 2002. http://www.epa.gov/performancetrack.

[8] Green Star. 19 July 2002. <http://www.greenstarinc.org/>.

VOLUNTARY PROGRAMS

Regulatory initiatives are not the only method in which industry, federal, state, and local governments can team up to prevent pollution. There are several voluntary programs that are also out to promote pollution prevention and get industry and the community involved. The following are some examples of voluntary pollution prevention programs.

Program	*How it Works*
Green Building Programs[9]	<ul><li>Promotes environmentally friendly construction of buildings</li><li>Providence of environmentally friendly homes.</li><li>Promotion of homes meeting environmental criteria.</li><li>Technical assistance/training</li></ul>
Energy Star[10]	<ul><li>Offers consumers and businesses energy efficient solutions</li><li>Solutions save money and provide for environmental protection.</li></ul>
WasteWise[11]	<ul><li>Open to all organizations</li><li>Promotes waste reduction through municipal solid waste elimination</li><li>Flexible — allows partners to design their own solid waste reduction programs tailored to their needs</li></ul>
Waste Prevention[12]	<ul><li>Involves altering the design, manufacture, purchase, or use of products</li><li>Reduce the amount and toxicity of waste</li><li>Helps shift the nation's emphasis from pollution cleanup to pollution avoidance</li></ul>

[9] "Community Green Building Programs." U.S. Department of Energy. 19 July 2002 <http://www.sustainable.doe.gov/buildings/gbprogrm.shtml>.

[10] Energy Star. 19 July 2002. <http://www.energystar.gov/default.shtml >.

[11] WasteWise. 14 August 2002, http://www.epa.gov/wastewise/about/overview.htm

[12] Waste Prevention. 14 August 2002, http://www.epa.gov/epaoswer/non-hw/reduce/prevent.htm

OTHER PROGRAMS

The federal, state, local, and non-profit plans for pollution prevention and environmental protection provide important regulations and strategies to reduce pollution. The identification and implementation of opportunities for pollution prevention integration in these regulations, plans, and strategies is critical to the success of all pollution prevention programs. To ensure the success of pollution prevention programs, government and other agencies must encourage and promote innovation (innovation of pollution-prevention technologies, innovation of pollution prevention methodologies, etc) and education. A key component to compliance is understanding why and how pollution control is imperative. Community leaders, "champions," should be identified and trained so that they can promote the importance, implications, significance, and benefits of pollution prevention in their communities.

Compliance assistance should be provided for small businesses and the non-regulated community to aid in understanding the regulations and beneficial pollution prevention practices. Promotion of innovation, fostering pollution prevention education, and training pollution prevention "champions" is costly. Funding support is crucial to the success of this plan. Pollution prevention and environmental justice have traditionally been referred to as federal priorities but have not been awarded sufficient and consistent budget appropriations to support full implementation and success. The adequacy of funding, innovation, education, and leadership are paramount for the success of the partnership between government and industry in thwarting pollution.

APPENDIX IV – POLLUTION PREVENTION WORK GROUP MEMBERS

DESIGNATED FEDERAL OFFICER
Sharon Weil. Austin (P2 Work Group)
Office of Pollution Prevention and Toxics
U.S. Environmental Protection Agency
1200 Pennsylvania Ave. NW (MC7406M)
Washington, DC 20460
Phone: (202) 564-8523
Fax: (202) 564-8528
E-mail: austin.sharon@epa.gov

Charles Lee   (NEJAC DFO)
Associate Director for Policy and Interagency
Liaison
Office of Environmental Justice
US Environmental Protection Agency
1300 Pennsylvania Ave. NW
Washington, DC 20460
Phone: 202-564-2597
Fax: (202) 501-1163
E-mail: lee.charles@epa.gov

WORK GROUP MEMBERS
* Denotes Liaison to NEJAC subcommittee

Nicholas Ashford
1 Amherst Street
Cambridge, Massachusetts 02139_4307
Phone: 617-253-8973
fax: 617-253-7140
E-mail: nashford@mit.edu

Charles (Chuck) Bennett, PhD
Senior Research Associate
Global Corporate Citizenship/
Townley Global Management Center
The Conference Board
845 Third Avenue
New York, NY 10022-6679
Phone: 212-339-0356
fax: 212-836-9717 (Fax)
E-mail: chuck.bennett@conference-board.org

CO-CHAIRS
Wilma Subra
LEAN Representative
Subra Company, Inc.
P. O. Box 9813
3814 Old Jeanerette Rd.
New Iberia, LA 70562
Phone: (337) 367-2216
Fax: (337) 367-2217
E-mail: SubraCom@aol.com

Kenneth J. Warren, Esq.
Chair of Environmental Department
Wolf, Block, Schorr and Solis-Cohen
1650 Arch Street, 22nd Floor
Philadelphia, PA 19103
Phone: (215) 977-2276
Fax: (215) 977-2334
E-mail: kwarren@wolfblock.com

Sue Briggum
Director of Environmental Affairs
Waste Management, Inc.
601 Pennsylvania Avenue, NW
North Building, Suite 300
Washington, DC 20004
Phone: 202-639-1219
Fax: 202-628-0400
E-mail: sbriggum@wm.com

Robin Morris Collin
PO Box 3185
Eugene, Oregon 97403
Phone: (541) 607-1072
Fax: 541-607-1072
E-mail: homemojo@aol.com

ADVANCING ENVIRONMENTAL JUSTICE THROUGH POLLUTION PREVENTION
NEJAC Pollution Prevention Report
Appendices
June 2003

Veronica Eady, Esq.*
Dept. of Urban & Environmental Policy &
Planning
Tufts University
97 Talbot Avenue
Medford, MA 02155
Tel. (617) 627-3394
Fax (617) 627-3377
E-mail: veronica.eady@tufts.edu

Ken Geiser
Massachusetts Toxics Use Reduction Institute
University of Massachusetts / Lowell
Lowell, MA 01854
Phone: 978-934-3275
Fax: 978-934-3050
E-mail: kgeiser@turi.org

Tom Goldtooth
Indigenous Environmental Network
P. O. Box 485
Bemjidi, MN 56619-0485
Phone: (218) 751-4967
Fax: (218) 751-0561
E-mail: ien@apc.ipc.org

LeAnn Herren
Industrial Ecology Program
University of South Carolina
School of the Environment
7th floor Burnes Building
Columbia, SC 29298
Phone: (803) 777-9061
Fax: (803)
E-mail: herren@environ.sc.edu

Debra Jacobson
Executive Director
Great Lakes Regional P2 Roundtable
1010 Jorie Blvd, Suite 12
Oak Brook, IL 60523
Phone: (630) 472-5019
Fax: (630) 472-5023
djacobso@wmrc.uiuc.edu

Neftali Garcia Martinez
Scientific and Technical Services
RR-2 Buzón
1722 Cupey Alto
San Juan, Puerto Rico 00926

Phone: (787) 292-0620
Fax: (787) 760-0496
E-mail: sctinc@coqui.net

Keith McCoy
Director, Environmental Quality
National Association of Manufacturers
1331 Pennsylvania Ave, NW Suite 600
Washington, DC 20004
(202) 637-3175
(202) 637-3182 (fax)
E-mail: kmccoy@nam.org

Tirso Moreno
Farmworkers Association of Florida
815 South Park Avenue
Apopka, FL 32703
(407) 886-5151
(407) 885-6644 (fax)
E-mail: tirsomoreno@hotmail.com

Theresa Peterson
3M Corporation
1101 15th Street NW
Suite 1100
Washington, DC 20005
Phone: (202) 331-6949
E-mail: thpeterson1@mmm.com

Coleen Poler *
Mole Lake Sokoagon Defense Committee
RR 1 Box 2015
Crandon, WI 54520
Phone: (715) 478-5033
Fax: (715) 365-8977
E-mail: polersdc@newnorth.net

Andrew Sawyers, PhD
Community Planning and Environmental Justice
Coordinator
Maryland Department of the Environment
1800 Washington Blvd
Baltimore, MD 21230
Phone: (410) 537-3411
Fax: (410) 537-3888
E-mail: asawyers@mde.state.md.us

Dean B. Suagee *
Vermont Law School
First Nations Environmental Law Program
Chelsea Street
South Royalton, VT 05068
Phone: (802) 763-8303 Ext. 2341
Fax: (802) 763-2940
E-mail: dsuagee@vermontlaw.edu

Connie Tucker
Southern Organizing Committee for
Economic and Social Justice
P.O. Box 10518
Atlanta, GA 30301
Phone: (404)-755-2855
Fax: (404) 755-0575
E-mail: cttucker@mindspring.com

Joanna Underwood
President
INFORM, Inc.
120 Wall Street, 16th Floor
New York, NY 10005
Phone: (212) 361-2400 x 222
fax: (212) 361-2412
E-mail: underwood@informinc.org

Richard Wells
President
The Lexington Group
110 Hartwell Avenue
Lexington, MA 02421-3136
Phone: (781) 674-7306
Fax: (781) 674-2851
E-mail: richard.wells@lexgrp.com

Dianne Wilkins*
Oklahoma Dept. of Environmental Quality
Pollution Prevention Program
P.O. Box 1677
Oklahoma City, OK 73101-1677
Phone: (405) 702-9128
Fax: (405) 702-9101
Fed Ex: 707 N. Robinson, 73102-6010
E-mail: Dianne.Wilkins@deq.state.ok.us

Donele Wilkins
Detroiter's Working for Environmental Justice
P.O. Box 14944
Detroit, MI 48214
Phone: (313) 821-1064
E-mail: dwdwej@msn.com

Consultant
Samara F. Swanston, ESQ.
205 W. 80th St., Apt. 1D
New York, New York 10024
Office (718) 384-3339
Home   (212) 799-1068
Cell: (917) 324-0541
E-mail: fotlah@aol.com

ADVANCING ENVIRONMENTAL JUSTICE THROUGH POLLUTION PREVENTION
NEJAC Pollution Prevention Report
Appendices
June 2003